W9-CFQ-618

CANAAN TOWN LIBRARY
P.O. BOX 368
CANAAN, NH 03741

62129√

# *New Hampshire*

# ICONS

CANAAN TOWN LIBRARY
P.O. BOX 368
CANAAN, NH 03741

DISCARD

# *New Hampshire*

# ICONS

## 50 CLASSIC SYMBOLS OF THE GRANITE STATE

Jennifer Smith-Mayo
and Matthew P. Mayo

**gpp**®

Guilford, Connecticut

To buy books in quantity for corporate use
or incentives, call **(800) 962–0973**
or e-mail **premiums@GlobePequot.com**.

Copyright © 2012 by Morris Book Publishing, LLC

ALL RIGHTS RESERVED. No part of this book may be reproduced or transmitted in any form by any means, electronic or mechanical, including photocopying and recording, or by any information storage and retrieval system, except as may be expressly permitted in writing from the publisher. Requests for permission should be addressed to Globe Pequot Press, Attn: Rights and Permissions Department, P.O. Box 480, Guilford, CT 06437.

Text design/layout: Casey Shain.

Photos by Jennifer Smith-Mayo, except where otherwise noted.
Text by Matthew P. Mayo.

Library of Congress Cataloging-in-Publication Data is available on file.

ISBN 978-0-7627-7144-8

Printed in the United States of America

10 9 8 7 6 5 4 3 2 1

*To Robin and Ed Hyland and family, lifelong friends.*
*To Erin Turner, for her kindness.*

# CONTENTS

# INTRODUCTION

*More than two decades ago,* we moved from Vermont to Maine, and in the years that followed, as we drove back and forth to visit family, we spent an inordinate amount of time in New Hampshire. More to the point, we spent much time passing *through* it, and, in the process, exploring every conceivable (and some inconceivable) east-west route, and in all manner of weather.

Having grown up in Vermont, as youths we were naturally well aware of New Hampshire, but other than occasional family forays and fishing jaunts along the Connecticut River (owned by New Hampshire, as it turns out), it was not until we were adults that we began to pay real attention to the state. Thankfully, it didn't take long for us to realize that the Granite State is its own special place with a long, rich history, a rugged, stunning landscape unmatched in New England, and a citizenry as friendly as they are fiercely proud of their chosen home.

And so for decades now we have explored New Hampshire, often with our dogs in tow, happily wandering off our usual routes, venturing far north and south, staying in tiny towns and big cities, and rubbing elbows with moose and bear and hunters and fishermen as we camped and fished near Colebrook and Conway. We've hiked throughout the White Mountains, where we never tire of watching immense, high clouds slowly drift, purpling the raw peaks, deep passes, and soft hills and valleys below. We've driven up Mount Washington, boated on Lakes Sunapee and Winnipesaukee, and shopped for books in Littleton and Keene. We've marveled at the wind-stripped crags of Crawford Notch. We've had world-class meals in fine hotels and even tastier sandwiches from mom-and-pop markets. We've visited the birthplaces and graves of war heroes and statesmen, and the homes of poets. And we've been to all the usual tourist haunts that are way too fun to pass up, among them Santa's Village, Six Gun City, and Clark's Trading Post.

We've grown so fond of New Hampshire, in fact, that we long ago gave up the excuse of visiting family in order to venture westward and lose ourselves (not literally . . . yet!) for a time hiking in her mountains (Franconia region being a particular favorite place), fishing in her rivers, and skiing and snowshoeing her slopes and meadows. Unsurprisingly, we have yet to repeat an adventure in the Granite State, and given her seemingly unlimited natural offerings, we doubt we ever will.

The White Mountains are a bold range—not for the faint of heart, but definitely for the adventurous. The same could be said for the entire state of New Hampshire. Her people—the ones who bend to a task and make it work, no matter the difficulties, be they farmers or professors, snowplow drivers or general store owners, ski-lift operators or housewives—are truly an independent lot, taking great pride in who they are and in what they do, such as being the first in the nation to cast votes in U.S. presidential primaries and elections.

They are also not impressed with an excess of government in their lives, and they keep a watchful eye on any such encroachments. As residents of the first colony to declare its independence from England (six months before the Declaration of Independence was signed), New Hampshirites still seem to take to heart General John Stark's immortal oath: "Live free or die; Death is not the worst of evils"—bold words that exemplify America's proud, optimistic spirit that refuses to consider defeat as an option, a sentiment as vital today as it was in 1809 when Stark penned it.

As with our similar books about Maine and Vermont, we suspected when we began this project that we would have no trouble finding fifty iconic elements that best symbolize the state of New Hampshire. And we were correct. The trouble started when we had to narrow down our several-hundred-symbol-long list. Unfortunately, many worthy people, places, and things were sacrificed, such as the Chinook dog breed, Famous Portsmouth Orange Cake, Polly's Pancake Parlor, Gilley's PM Lunch, or the fact that Peterborough's was the first publicly funded library in the United States, or that the first potato planted in the U.S. was at Londonderry in 1719, or that Moultonboro's Old Country Store may well be the oldest mercantile in America, or that Littleton's Lahout's is the oldest ski shop in the country, or that Concord teacher Christa McAuliffe was selected as the first private citizen to venture into space, or that New Hampshire is also known as the Switzerland of America and the Mother of Rivers. . . . We could go on (and perhaps we will one day, in a second volume), but for now, we hope the fifty iconic elements represented here collectively give readers a sense of the rich and amazing historic, geographic, and cultural breadth of the Granite State, a place (and people) truly like no other.

Perhaps we'll see you in Portsmouth . . . or Pittsburg—or any place in between!

Cheers,
The Mayos

NEW HAMPSHIRE ICONS

# LIVE FREE OR DIE

*Most Granite Staters* know, and take justifiable pride in, their state's official motto, *Live free or die.* But not all know its origins . . .

In his ninety-three years, John Stark showed more mettle than most men. This lifelong resident of New Hampshire was born in Londonderry, and as a child moved to Derryfield (now Manchester), where he lived for the rest of his days.

As a young man, he was captured by Abenaki warriors who were so impressed with his bravery that the tribe adopted him. Stark also fought in the French and Indian War, but is most renowned for his activity in Revolutionary War battles, among them the Siege of Boston and the Battle of Bunker Hill. Between soldiering excursions, he fathered eleven children with his wife, Elizabeth "Molly" Stark. In 1777, as a brigadier general of the New Hampshire militia, Stark's men won the pivotal Battle of Bennington, where he famously rallied them by saying, "There are your enemies, the Red Coats and the Tories. They are ours, or this night Molly Stark sleeps a widow!"

*Visit General Stark's grave and learn more about New Hampshire's foremost Revolutionary War hero: Friends of Stark Park, www .friendsofstark park.org*

In 1809, at the age of eighty-one and unable to travel, General Stark sent a letter to a gathering of his fellow Bennington Battle veterans, which he closed with the words, "Live free or die: Death is not the worst of evils." It took until 1945, but the state of New Hampshire adopted the paraphrased slogan, *Live free or die,* as its state motto, now considered the most striking and memorable of all official state mottos.

General John Stark is honored throughout the nation with statues, parks, schools, and monuments bearing his name or likeness, including the larger-than-life bronze at Stark Park, in his hometown of Manchester, where he and his wife, Molly, are buried.

In 1971, the New Hampshire legislature voted to replace the word SCENIC on the state's license plates with Stark's bold motto, where it remains today. And thus, the impressive General John Stark continues to inspire countless New Hampshirites daily, more than two centuries after he committed his proud oath to paper.

THIS MONUMENT
THE GIFT OF
GENERAL

MAJOR GENERAL JOHN STARK

# CONNECTICUT RIVER

In New Hampshire's far-northern reaches, the headwaters of New England's longest river, at 410 miles in length, begins humbly at Fourth Connecticut Lake (really more of a pond), just a few feet from the Quebec border. From there it drains 11,000 square miles of land as it travels southward to the Atlantic. Lived alongside and revered for 10,000 years by Native Americans, in 1614 the river was officially "discovered" by Dutch explorer Adriaen Block, who named it the "Fresh River." The Algonquin called it *quinetucket,* which translates as "long tidal river," and in later years the bastardized French version came out as "Connecticut."

The Connecticut River forms New Hampshire's border with Vermont. But despite common assumptions, New Hampshire's true western edge is not the center of the river, but on the Vermont side at the low-water mark, which means that New Hampshire owns the Connecticut River as it runs adjacent to Vermont. Fifty-four tributaries feed into the Connecticut River before she enters Long Island sound at Old Lyme,

*Learn all about the mighty river and its environs at Connecticut River Watershed Council: www .ctriver.org*

Connecticut, where her significant amount of silt impedes navigation.

The Connecticut River was first spanned by a bridge in 1785, between Walpole, New Hampshire, and Bellows Falls, Vermont. Later, the river became a major thoroughfare for some of the nation's biggest log drives of the late nineteenth and early twentieth centuries. In March of 1936, the river flooded to 20 feet above its banks, and caused $500 million in damages, killed 171 people, and left 430,000 homeless.

Today, after major reclamation efforts following decades of pollution from factories and excessive logging, the Connecticut River is among the most popular recreation waterways in the Northeast. It is home to healthy populations of brook, rainbow, and brown trout, as well as smallmouth bass, shad, carp, catfish, American eel, and striper. And the vast Connecticut River Valley is home to a wide array of wildlife, including bald eagles, salamanders, shellfish, fox, deer, and bear. A few farmers and their cows have been spotted along her banks, too.

# NO SALES TAX

Shopping for booze at any one of the sixty-five New Hampshire Liquor & Wine Outlets has long been a favorite pastime for travelers headed to or from their New Hampshire vacations. The superstores are owned and run by the New Hampshire State Liquor Commission, and in high summer the multi-acre parking lots of the larger outlets (particularly along Interstate 93) are jam-packed with cars, trucks, motorcycles, campers, and motor homes towing SUVs. Inside, the aisles of the massive, inviting liquor and wine warehouses teem with tanned adults pushing shopping carts packed with all manner of mixers, wine boxes and bottles, whiskies of the world, and more—mostly tax-free. (While there are certain taxes on alcohol in New Hampshire, none are apparently too prohibitive.)

That's because New Hampshire is one of only five states that does not have a general sales tax on goods and services (the others are Alaska, Delaware, Montana, and Oregon). The lack of a New Hampshire sales tax is a great enticement

*Thirsty? Drop on by: www.liquorand wineoutlets.com*

for folks from Vermont and Maine to venture over the border when it comes time to upgrade their washer and dryer, or better yet, to buy a new pickup truck.

Not only is there no general sales tax, but at the state and local levels, New Hampshirites—whose median household income as of 2010 was $60,441 (sixth highest in the nation)—are also not taxed on personal income. But that doesn't mean folks in New Hampshire don't pay the piper. Taxes are paid on meals and lodging (8 percent), vehicles, gas/diesel (19.6 percent per gallon), state roads (think *tolls*), and on investment income. The state also collects significant taxes on motor fuels, tobacco products, in-state pari-mutuel betting, and a variety of state-run lottery programs.

All of this seemingly low-tax/no-tax status has resulted in many local communities enforcing some of the highest property taxes in the nation, making New Hampshire forty-ninth out of fifty states in its combined state and local tax burden. And that can be mighty taxing.

# NEW HAMPSHIRE HIGHLAND GAMES

*It might surprise folks* to learn that New Hampshire is home to a brawny contingent of Scots, Scottish supporters, and fans of bagpipe music—at once the single most loved and reviled musical instrument in the world. Yet only 4.8 percent of New Hampshire's population of 1,316,000 is of Scots descent, and 2.7 percent are Scots-Irish. So why such a yen for all things Gaelic? Perhaps it's because each September, the largest Scottish cultural festival in the Northeast takes place at Loon Mountain Ski Resort in Lincoln. In fact, 2012 marks the thirty-sixth annual New Hampshire Highland Games, presented by the New Hampshire Gathering of the Scottish Clans, Inc. This not-for-profit organization is "dedicated to the furtherance of the music, dance, athletics, and customs of the Scottish people and the continuance of the Gaelic culture."

The festival's revelries include a Gathering of the Clans, participated in by more than sixty clans and Scottish societies, along with competitions and performances featuring *clarsach* (Gaelic for "small harp"), fiddle, Highland

**Don yer kilt and grab yer pipes! See you in September at Loon Mountain Ski Resort, Lincoln: www.nh scot.org**

dance, piping, drumming, thirty pipe bands, athletic competitions, sheepdog trials, and a living history area representing Scotia's long-ago Highland clans.

The New Hampshire Highland Games has also hosted world championships in the Heavy Events, those manly athletic competitions in which big, burly men strap on hernia belts over their kilts and growl and bark as they hoist massive wooden poles (*cabers*), fling the hammer, and throw the stone. Another not-to-be-missed event is whisky tasting (the correct spelling if you're talking about the stuff from Scotland—otherwise, it's mere "whiskey").

In May 1995, the New Hampshire legislature passed a bill granting the State of New Hampshire its own official tartan. Designed by a New Hampshire hand weaver and registered through the authorities in Scotland who oversee such things, the colors in the unique tartan represent various aspects of the state. Among other uses, it is the pattern used in the kilts worn by Lincoln's police officers when they work to keep the Scottish hordes contained at the annual New Hampshire Highland Games.

# THE GRANITE STATE

New Hampshire earned its bold nickname in 1825 with a song marking American Revolutionary War hero General Lafayette's visit to Concord: "He comes, by fond entreaties moved, The Granite State to see." Yet, for a state that takes justifiable pride in its extensive granite deposits, it wasn't until the seemingly late date of May 31, 1985, that granite was designated as the official state rock of New Hampshire.

Granite is one of the strongest rocks known to man because the minerals of which it is composed—notably quartz and feldspar—interlock, allowing the resultant rock to sustain tremendous pressure. Granite weathers slowly and retains chiseled decoration for a long time. In 1810, granite was used in the construction of the New Hampshire state prison in Concord, and then the prisoners bent their backs to the task of carving up 3,000 tons of granite for the State House.

The state's rock-heavy history is nearly synonymous with one company: Swenson Granite Works. Now run by the fifth generation of Swensons, it's been in the business since 1883. Based

*Granite for all occasions: Swenson Granite Works, 369 North State Street, Concord; (603) 225-4322; www.swensongranite.com*

on Rattlesnake Hill and overlooking the state's capital city of Concord, it's the oldest surviving quarry in New Hampshire. The hill was home, in its quarrying heyday at the turn of the nineteenth to the twentieth century, to forty-four companies employing stone workers or "granite boys" from all over the world.

Today, Swenson also owns the world's largest quarry, Rock of Ages, in Barre, Vermont, making Swenson Granite Works the biggest quarrier and granite-product manufacturer in North America. Among the numerous structures that boast Swenson-supplied granite are the Brooklyn Bridge, the Pentagon, St. Patrick's Cathedral, and others.

But Concord doesn't have a historic lock on the state's granite supply. Milford, still known as "Granite Town," supplied granite for the pillars of the U.S. Treasury building, featured in the sketch on the U.S. $10 bill. And Madison is home to the Madison Boulder; one of the largest glacial erratics in the world, it measures 83 by 23 by 37 feet and weighs 5,000 tons. Now that's a lot of granite.

# FIRST-IN-THE-NATION
# PRESIDENTIAL PRIMARY

For 99 percent of the time, the residents of two tiny New Hampshire towns go about their business unobserved by the rest of the world. But every four years, the eyes of the nation focus on big-city journalists wearing new plaid flannel shirts and their best wry smiles as they cover the doings in Dixville Notch, way up in Coos County, and Hart's Location, in Carroll County.

That's because, since these towns sport less than a hundred citizens each, per state law they are allowed to open their polls at midnight and then close them again when all registered voters have cast their ballots, a rather brief process. (In Dixville Notch, it takes place in the Ballot Room of the Balsams Grand Resort Hotel.) This makes New Hampshire's primary and presidential vote the very first in the American presidential-election process that takes place every four years, a tradition and distinction the state has held since 1920, although it has held a primary since 1916. Its significance and impact on races didn't reach critical mass until the 1952 race, after New Hampshire tinkered with

*Setting national trends in small-town New Hampshire: Hart's Location: www.harts location.com*

*Dixville Notch: www.thebalsams .com/history*

its ballot-access laws in an effort to get more people to the voting booths.

In 1988, when Iowa's caucus was gaining increased national attention, then-governor of New Hampshire, John H. Sununu, famously said in defense of his state's first-in-the-nation primary, "The people of Iowa pick corn; the people of New Hampshire pick presidents."

And how influential are the votes from these diminutive places? The state used to be largely Republican in bent. Though from 1992 through 2008, it supported all the Democratic candidates, save for 2000, when it supported Bush, then didn't in 2004—the only state to *not* follow up on its previous opinion.

In truth, the state's history of choosing winners has been a mixed bag, as with any process involving votes. But that doesn't seem to slow the hordes of journalists from descending on the state every four years to offer up their knowing smiles and surmises about how it is these small-town voters can carry so much clout. . . . Ayuh.

# STONE WALLS

New Hampshire's most revered poet, Robert Frost, once quoted a seventeenth-century proverb in his poem, "Mending Wall": "Good fences make good neighbors," using the ancient walls on his Derry farm as inspiration. The earliest stone walls in the state replaced the earliest fences, easily built, zigzag wood-rail structures. As the land became cleared, trees were needed for firewood, construction of homes and barns, and truss work. Eventually, the nearest usable trees were gone, and the rail fences rotted, but the need for walls remained. Fortunately for the Granite State, New Hampshire never suffered from a lack of stones.

Indeed, the abundance of rocks on New Hampshire farms meant that a farmer who found himself with an excess wasn't necessarily an unhappy man. He could use the plentiful material to build foundations for his house, barns, and outbuildings; to construct boundary and animal fencing and chimneys; to line wells; and even to sell to farmers whose land wasn't so blessed with stones.

The sale of stone was big business, especially during the heyday of New

New Hampshire
Stone Walls:
www.stonewall
pros.com

Stone Wall
Initiative:
www.stonewall
.uconn.edu

England stone-wall building—roughly 1775 to 1825—which coincided with the expansion of settlers into northern New England. Stone walls constructed during this period were often built by professional freelance stonemasons.

In 1871, the USDA measured 252,539 miles of stone walls in New England and New York—enough to encircle the Earth at the equator ten times, and the labor involved could have built the Egyptian pyramids a hundred times over. But though they are still abundant in the state, many old stone walls are disappearing. In 2009, due to an alarming rise in stone-wall theft (the handsome, weathered stones are highly prized items by downcountry landscapers), New Hampshire governor John Lynch enhanced legislation on the books since 1791, awarding "treble damages" to parties who have experienced stone-wall theft.

Nowadays, it's as easy to stumble on an old stone wall in New Hampshire while walking in the woods as it is to find one still in use at the edges of a field. Then again, those woods might well have been where sheep once grazed in full sun.

# PORTSMOUTH NAVAL SHIPYARD

*In 2002, the U.S.* government-ment decided that the site of the Portsmouth (as in New Hampshire) Naval Shipyard—Seavey's Island—belongs to the state of Maine, and *not* New Hampshire. So, why is it still named after New Hampshire's most famous historic seaport city? Well, the Portsmouth Naval Shipyard wasn't always located in Maine. In 2000, two centuries after the shipyard was established, the state of New Hampshire filed a lawsuit against the state of Maine in hopes of having its border verified as running to the Maine shore of the Piscataqua River.

But New Hampshire lost its lawsuit because, in 1977, it had won a similar suit over lobstering rights, which stated that the true border ran down the middle of the waterway. And so, though federally owned and named after a city in New Hampshire, Portsmouth Naval Shipyard now formally resides in the town of Kittery, Maine.

In 1800, the U.S. government, owner of the land, conjoined five small islands making up what is known today as Seavey's Island. By 1815, the shipyard had floated its first commission, a war-

Learn more about this Maine-based New Hampshire icon at Portsmouth Naval Shipyard: www.navsea.navy .mil/shipyards/ portsmouth; www.portsnaval museums.com

ship named USS *Washington,* bristling with seventy-four guns, and it hasn't ceased operations since. During World War I, the shipyard began constructing submarines, employing 5,000 civilians. Its ranks swelled to 25,000 during World War II, when the yard manufactured seventy submarines. It launched its last sub, the nuclear-powered USS *Sand Lance*, in 1969.

Today, this oldest continuously operating shipyard in the U.S. Navy employs 4,500 civilians, and 100 naval officers and enlistees are based there. And though fifty of its buildings are on the National Register of Historic Places, the facility is capable of handling the most cutting-edge repairs and refits on all active submarine classes.

Despite the outcome of the 2002 court case ruling in favor of Maine as owner of the land on which it sits, New Hampshire's 2006 Legislative Session reaffirmed in House Joint Resolution 1 the state's sovereignty over Seavey's Island and the Piscataqua River as being "within the boundaries of the state of New Hampshire," thus stating a historical claim to ownership. Defiant? You bet.

# COVERED BRIDGES

Of the 750 or so covered bridges found today throughout the United States, a respectable 54 still decorate New Hampshire's landscape. At its covered-bridge heyday in the mid-nineteenth century, the Granite State was home to more than 400 of the impressive structures. Thankfully, the New Hampshire state legislature recognized their historical significance and enacted a law protecting New Hampshire's remaining covered bridges.

But why cover them in the first place? Since the structures were all hand-built of wood, they represented a significant investment in time, money, and materials, so it made practical sense to roof the bridges to keep damaging weather out—and lovers concealed. Also known as "kissing bridges," covered bridges provide sparking couples a quick opportunity to steal a smooch while escaping the gaze of nosy neighbors.

New Hampshire's robust collection of covered bridges is a colorful lot, with names such as Blow-Me-Down (in Cornish), Bump (one of Campton's three covered bridges), and the Honeymoon Bridge (in Jackson). The open-lattice

*Learn more about New Hampshire's historic collection:*
*www.nh.gov/ nhdhr/bridges*

*www.covered bridgesite.com/ nh/nh_home.html*

*www.dalejtravis .com/bridge/ bridgenh.htm*

Ashuelot Bridge, in Winchester, is the state's most elaborate-looking, but the Cornish-Windsor Bridge is the crown jewel of New Hampshire's vast collection. The current bridge, the fourth on the site (its predecessors were destroyed by flooding), was originally built in 1866. At 460 feet, composed of two spans supported in the middle, it is the longest covered bridge in the United States, and the longest two-span covered bridge in the world. The mighty bridge crosses the fabled Connecticut River where, from the Vermont side, it is called the Windsor-Cornish Bridge. Given that its original construction cost was $9,000 in 1866, it is a testament to New Hampshire's dedication to its historic past that in 1989, the famously frugal state reconstructed the deteriorating structure at a cost of $4,450,000.

At the other extreme, the Prentiss Bridge (1791), aka the Drewsville Bridge, is the shortest covered bridge in the state, with an overall length of 34 feet, 6 inches. One of the cutest covered bridges anywhere, its original cost was six pounds, which today might buy a handful of nails and a few two-by-fours.

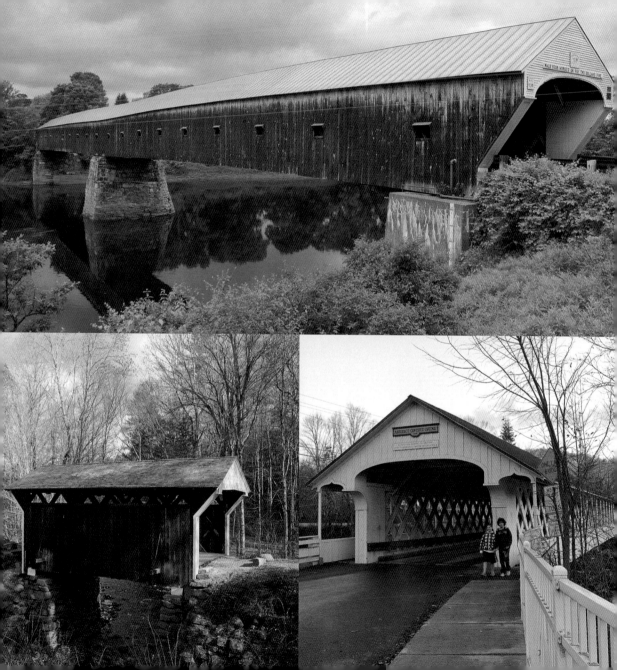

# SNOWMOBILING

*Way back in 1913,* West Ossipee resident and Ford automobile dealer Virgil D. White converted a Motel T into something that could run in the snow, using his own fabricated tracks and skis. It's a safe bet that Mr. White had no idea of his invention's eventual impact when he received a patent on his conversion kit, or when he coined and copyrighted the name "snowmobile." But all of his efforts added up to make New Hampshire the birthplace of snowmobiling, today a nationwide, multimillion-dollar industry.

In 1922, White began selling his kits via Ford dealers, and soon, snow-converted autos were roaming all over the North Country, including school buses, taxis, milk vans, and log trucks. Today, from south to north, east to west, over hills and through valleys, across rivers, lakes, and fields, members of the 115 clubs that make up the New Hampshire Snowmobile Association (NHSA) maintain 6,800-plus miles of groomed trails.

Lest anyone doubt the importance of the sport to

*The snowy backcountry is calling! New Hampshire Snowmobile Association: (603) 273-0220; www.nhsa.com*

*New Hampshire Snowmobile Museum: Bear Brook State Park, off Route 28, Allenstown; (603) 809-8700; info@nhsnow mobilemuseum .com; www.hsnow mobilemuseum .com*

the state, the total impact of snowmobiling on the state's economy in a single recent season was more than $1 billion. Spending by snowmobilers accounts for 1 percent of the state's gross product and more than 10 percent of all money spent in New Hampshire by travelers. No snowmobile? No problem: There are numerous places throughout the state where winter visitors can rent machines. They may not be Model Ts, but they will get snow-hungry folks from A to B in grand shape, stunning scenery guaranteed.

Despite the popularity of high-tech snowmobiles with laser-like looks and high-octane engines capable of super speeds, the National Model T Ford Snowmobile Club ensures that the sport's past is not forgotten. It holds its annual two-day gathering in Gilford in February, sponsored in part by the New Hampshire Snowmobile Museum Association, which also holds an annual meeting the following week at its museum in Allenstown.

# THE DEERFIELD FAIR

In a time when every town seems to be working extra hard to distinguish itself from all the others, the demure burg of Deerfield, population 4,400, proudly offers what it calls "New England's oldest family fair," widely regarded as one of the finest in the state. Located just 20 miles from Manchester and 65 miles from Boston, Deerfield's four-day event, still largely agricultural, was established in 1876, with 2012 marking its 136th year.

In a variety of polls, the Deerfield Fair comes out far ahead of others, with high marks for its cleanliness; old-time, wholesome family fun; and its emphasis on the agricultural heritage of the region and the state. The much-anticipated event kicks off every year in late September, with an opening ceremony at 9 a.m., then launches into the highly attended ox and horse pulls, dairy and sheep shows, and poultry and fowl judging.

There are numerous works for show and sale by artisans, and halls are filled with 4-H exhibits, and floral, fruit, and vegetable com-

*It's never too late to plan a visit to the Deerfield Fair, 34 Stage Road, Deerfield; (603) 463-7421; deerfieldfair @deerfieldfair .com; www.deer fieldfair.com*

*New Hampshire Association of Fairs & Expositions: www.nhfairs.com*

petitions, including monster pumpkins that top out at more than a thousand pounds. Don't forget the demolition derby, the Ms. Deerfield Fair pageant, square-dancing demonstrations, scavenger hunts, ventriloquists, magicians, famous singers, pig scrambles, tractor pulls, concessions galore, and tasty treats including blooming onions, hot mulled cider, homemade apple crisp, deep-fried everything, Maine lobster, pulled pork, bison burgers, spicy sausages, and french fries, too.

The Deerfield Fair is one of the few in New England with plenty of elbow room, numerous areas for relaxation, and lots of trees under which sun-weary visitors can find a shady spot. Historians in the family might want to visit the 1930s CCC-built building, now the Deerfield Fair's museum, housing a repository of items from the fair's long and interesting past. And yes, there's even a midway with rides and games. But the true mark of the Deerfield Fair's enduring success? People leave tired and smiling.

# THE WHITE BIRCH

*It seems that* New Hampshire has a preoccupation with the color white: the White Mountains, white-tailed deer, white snow, and white birches. The latter was selected by the state legislature in 1947 as the official state tree, and for good reason, as the Granite State is peppered with groves of magnificent specimens. The Shelburne Birches, on Route 2 in Shelburne—perhaps the most famous grove in the state—has been undergoing a bit of forestry renovation that includes thinning to encourage new birch growth. But this magical stretch of road is nonetheless impressive at any time of year, even more enhanced in the fall with its colorful foliage, and is maintained as a memorial park, dedicated with a plaque to honor local veterans.

American white birch—*Betula papyrifera* (also known as white birch, paper birch, and canoe birch)—is a distinctive species native to North America. It can reach up to 60 feet tall, though there have been much larger exceptions. And, as its

Handsome . . . The Shelburne Birches, Route 2, in Shelburne near Gorham . . . and tasty, too! The Crooked Chimney, 11 Randall Road, Lee; www.crooked chimneysyrup .com

8 Ounces of
Pure New Hampshire
BIRCH SYRUP
Refrigerate After Opening
Produced and Bottled by:
The Crooked Chimney
11 Randall Road, Lee, NH 03861
www.crookedchimneysyrup.com

various names imply, the tree is used in numerous ways. The bark from larger specimens was highly prized by Native Americans as a writing material, and also for use in constructing their distinctive birch-bark canoes, though white birches don't typically take on their distinctive papery white bark until roughly five years of age.

Considered imperiled in certain other states, New Hampshire's birch population is a healthy, multiuse species. A few folks even tap New Hampshire's birch trees, much as one might a maple, among them The Crooked Chimney, which makes tasty birch syrup that resembles dark maple syrup in color and consistency. White birches are lovely to look at, produce grand colors in the fall, offer dappled shading in the summer, and sound soothing in a gentle breeze. The bark is a preferred staple for moose and white-tailed deer in winter, and the wood, when seasoned, burns long and warm, and is also used in making furniture, Popsicle sticks, and wafer board.

# STRAWBERY BANKE

Strawbery Banke (with one "r" in "Strawbery") gained its unusual name from English settlers early in the seventeenth century who were fond of the wild berries growing in the region. But that's the least unusual thing about this outdoor living history museum. It's also one of New England's earliest waterfront neighborhoods, located smack-dab in the middle of the historic district of famed seaport town, Portsmouth. Consisting of forty-two buildings, dating from the seventeenth through the twentieth century—the oldest of the Banke's structures dates from 1695—most are still on their original foundations, one of the many distinctions that makes Strawbery Banke unique among other such outdoor museums.

The site was originally chosen by English settlers in 1630 because of its promise as a safe harbor at the mouth of the Piscataqua River. Today, Strawbery Banke represents four centuries of New England seaport life, from colonial times through World War II. A living museum since 1963, Strawbery Banke was saved from the frenzy of urban renewal sweeping the nation, and its preserva-

*History lives at Strawbery Banke Museum: Open daily 10 a.m. to 5 p.m., May 1– October 31; 14 Hancock Street, Portsmouth; (603) 433-1100; www.strawbery banke.org*

tion helped facilitate the creation of the National Historic Preservation Act of 1966.

Visitors can stop off at the candy counter in the Marden-Abbott Store and see a genuine cooper at work at the Dinsmore Shop. The potters' studio offers live demonstrations, and the Wheelwright House shows colonial hearth cookery and traditional weaving. Many of these locations are tended by docents in period costume and in character, ensuring that visitors experience the location's full historical flavor. The museum is also noted nationwide for its Historic Landscapes Department, which maintains four centuries' worth of historic gardens filled with organic, heirloom plantings. Strawbery Banke also owns and operates the last three machines in the United States that make cut copper clench nails, much sought after by boatbuilders and hobbyists.

Self-guided tours of Strawbery Banke have never been easier now that there's an app for that. Yep . . . anyone with a smartphone can listen to narration about long-ago life in this still-thriving waterfront community.

# KELLERHAUS

*In 1906, Otto G. Keller* dipped his first bonbon, and in 1920, the Keller family began scooping out its own homemade ice cream. Since then, Kellerhaus has been satisfying the significant sweet tooth of Granite Staters of all ages, and is New Hampshire's oldest commercial candy maker *and* its oldest ice-cream maker.

Visitors to Kellerhaus, overlooking Weirs Beach and Lake Winnipesaukee, find eleven rooms brimming with gift items and confectionary goodness, including an inexhaustible supply of handmade bonbons, turtles, butter crunch, pecan bark, cherry cordials, nonpareils, peanut-butter cups, and fudge. And don't forget peanut brittle, rock candy, ginger chews, and specialty sweets (Kellerhaus is one of the few confectioners in the world that still makes its own ribbon candy by hand). It also offers a huge assortment of New Hampshire–made maple treats, and a vast selection of homemade jellies and jams.

Would a sweets shop have a salad bar? Heck no, but Kellerhaus is home to the Ice Cream Buffet, where, for forty years, visitors have topped their

*Never was there a sweeter spot to visit: Kellerhaus, 259 Endicott Street North, Weirs Beach; (603) 366-4466; www.kellerhaus .com*

choice of ice cream any way they want to, with hot fudge, butterscotch, or strawberry sauces, fresh whipped cream, candy sprinkles, nuts, macaroon crunch, M&Ms, Oreos, and more. Plus, every Wednesday is $1 Cone Day, and on weekends, Kellerhaus serves a popular breakfast, including its famous Waffle Smorgasbord.

In 2004, Mary Ellen and David Dutton purchased the business (which included the facilities, the recipes, and secret confectioners' techniques), and continue to operate it as their predecessors did, maintaining the high quality of the candies and ice cream while adding new and unique twists to the offerings.

It's rare that visitors leave the 5,000-square-foot emporium empty-handed or without a smile (there's even a player piano inside). Customers always seem to need a little something for the road, and perhaps a gift basket filled with candles, stuffed animals, greeting cards, toys, holiday gifts (clothing, jewelry, books, ornaments, maple goodies, coffee)—all excellent reasons why people visit Kellerhaus, to be sure. But they really come for the candy and ice cream.

# THE SEACOAST

*For such a diminutive* stretch of coastline—a mere 18 miles, the shortest of any U.S. state—New Hampshire remains fiercely proud of her wee Atlantic strip. Referred to in-state as the Seacoast Region, it's New Hampshire's southeasternmost spot. And a staggering amount of activities, attractions, and dining and shopping opportunities are packed into such a modest stretch, beginning in the south where New Hampshire meets Salisbury, Massachusetts, then inching toward Hampton Beach. All anyone could ask for in a summer beach-resort town, it's rated as one of the top ten resort values in the United States. And the beach itself? It's right at the top of the cleanest-beaches-in-America list.

Continuing northeastward to New Hampshire's border with Kittery, Maine, we reach the Piscataqua River, long a region of contention between the two states. Though Maine won the U.S. Supreme Court coin toss in 2002, New Hampshire still proudly (and not a little stubbornly) claims sovereign rights to ownership of Seavey's Island, on which sits Portsmouth Naval Shipyard.

Head for the shore! Hampton Beach awaits: www.hamptonbeach.org

And so does Portsmouth: www.portsmouthchamber.org

In addition to its 18 mainland miles of coastline, New Hampshire lays claim to an additional 5 by measuring the collective shorelines of its holdings in the Gulf of Maine—namely the Isles of Shoals, which include White, Seavey, Star, and Lunging Islands, the latter of which is said to be where notorious pirate Blackbeard buried a mother lode of pillaged bars of silver (notwithstanding the fact that there's hardly topsoil enough to sink a spade).

Portsmouth's Strawbery Banke is one of the most impressive outdoor living history museums in the United States, just a stone's throw from the island of New Castle, at the mouth of the Piscataqua River estuary. Originally occupied by the British in 1632, a fort in one form or another has since stood on that spot, the most recent of which, rebuilt during the Civil War, is a three-tiered brute built of granite (naturally). Today, it is a state-run park called Fort Constitution Historic Site, on the grounds of which sits Portsmouth Harbor Light, a 48-foot lighthouse dating from 1878, which is also open for tours—and is allegedly haunted.

# MACK'S APPLES

*Moose Hill Orchards,* Londonderry, home to award-winning Mack's Apples, is New Hampshire's oldest family-run apple orchard, farmed by the Mack family since 1732. This 400-acre farm, the oldest you-pick orchard in the state, devotes one hundred acres to apples. That's a whole lot of what colonial folks called "winter bananas," and in a whole lot of varieties—thirty of them, including Jersey Mac, Tydeman, Paula Red, Ginger Gold, Jonamac, Gala, Honeycrisp, Macoun, Mutsu, and a host of others.

Half the fun of heading to Mack's is in the picking. It's an annual outing for many families, who often bring picnic lunches and tramp the hiking trails to make a day of it. Throughout apple season, which begins in mid-August and runs through mid-October, Mack's presses its own cider, holds contests and sampling events, and hosts the perennially popular Mack's Annual Apple Pie Contest. And all of this tasty goodness is available at the orchard's farm stand, The Farm Market, which also sells New Hampshire maple syrup, local honey, and locally

*Come pickin' time, head for Mack's Apples: 230 Mammoth Road, Londonderry; Apple Hotline (603) 432-3456; www.macks apples.com*

*Londonderry Trailways: www.londonderry trails.org*

made pies, jams, and jellies. Should visitors wish to share some appley goodness with the folks back home, Mack's gladly ships gift-boxed apples, syrup, and other goodies, anywhere in the United States.

But Mack's isn't an autumn-only venue. The farm stand serves ice cream from April through mid-September, and miles of walking trails throughout the bucolic grounds are maintained by Londonderry Trailways, which also grooms them in the winter for cross-country skiing—and there's no charge for using them.

In addition to apples, Mack's grows peaches, pears, squash, and 35 acres of pick-your-own pumpkins. Good thing, as the mighty mellow melons are the official state fruit of New Hampshire, declared as such in 2006 by the New Hampshire legislature. But have no fear, the humble apple is hardly forgotten, since on September 6, 2010, the same legislature deemed apple cider to be the official state beverage. No doubt Mack's—and the other fine orchards throughout New Hampshire—had a little something to do with that.

U-PACK Select your own right from the bin

FARMING IN LONDONDERRY SINCE 1732

MARKET DAILY 9-6

# THE MUSIC HALL

Built in 1878, Portsmouth's Music Hall, a 906-seat Victorian theater, is the oldest operating theater in the state, and the fourteenth-oldest in the United States. It's seen its share of impressive names tromp the boards, including luminaries ranging from Mark Twain and Buffalo Bill Cody to Wynton Marsalis and Joshua Bell.

After nearly a century of ups and downs in ownership and upkeep, in 1987, the nonprofit Friends of the Music Hall rescued the grand old lady from the brink of demolition, and has since undertaken award-winning restorations that mingle the modern—efficient LED lighting—with her late-nineteenth-century architectural impressiveness, such as her stunningly reconstructed $2.2 million, lobby, bar, and concession area makeover.

The recently redone interior, a spot-on accurate reflection of Victorian theaters, features ceiling paintings, impressive plasterwork, and an amazing revived proscenium arch. The theater also retains its original hardwood flooring and horseshoe-shaped balcony, and plans are afoot to restore the staircases

*Who—and what—is coming next? Find out at 28 Chestnut Street, Portsmouth; Box Office (603) 436-2400; Film Hotline (603) 436-9900; www.themusic hall.org*

and upper balcony. The Music Hall staff is also proud of its "world-class" restrooms, which feature brick and tile salvaged during the reconstruction, and are fitted with unexpected artistic flourishes.

In exploring the extent of damage to the theater's water-stained ceiling, elaborate artwork was discovered beneath four layers of paint. Although too costly to fully restore, it has been painstakingly re-created. Though renovations are ongoing—part of a long-term, multimillion-dollar improvement plan—the Founders Lobby, with modern access and amenities, opened to the public in September 2008.

Today, the Music Hall continues its longtime role, hosting acts in music, theater, and dance, as well as a film series, and sees more than 100,000 attendees each season. It is also one of downtown Portsmouth's largest employers, and is a nonprofit organization supported by 3,000 members, 300 business supporters, and 40 community partners.

The Music Hall also runs The Loft, a chic performance space just around the corner.

# DANIEL WEBSTER

*One of New Hampshire's* most-famous sons, orator, statesman, and lawyer Daniel Webster was born in a log cabin in Salisbury (now Franklin) on January 8, 1782, one of fourteen siblings. As a youth, he attended both Phillips Exeter Academy in Exeter and Dartmouth College, before apprenticing with a local lawyer.

From such humble beginnings, Webster would go on to serve as a U.S. congressman from two states (New Hampshire and Massachusetts), the only man ever to do so. He also held the office of secretary of state under three U.S. presidents, Harrison, Tyler, and Fillmore. But it is his silver tongue for which Webster remains best known. In 1830, he delivered what has been called "the most eloquent speech ever delivered in Congress," his famous "Reply to Hayne." And in a celebrated short story, "The Devil and Daniel Webster," by Stephen Vincent Benét, a New Hampshire farmer sells his soul to the devil and Daniel Webster defends him—successfully, of course.

In contrast with his impressive professional achievements, in his private life

*Daniel Webster Birthplace State Historic Site: 131 North Road, Franklin; (603) 934-5057*

Webster was a poor manager of money, drank to excess, and supported various mistresses. He came to an ignoble end on October 24, 1852, in Marshfield, Massachusetts, when he hit his head after falling from his horse.

Webster's name and likeness grace colleges, parks, and buildings all over the United States. In New Hampshire, his statue stands at the State House, a mountain in the Whites is named for him, and his home place is a National Historic Landmark. The town of Webster is named for him, as is Webster Lake in Franklin, and U.S. Route 3 in New Hampshire is also known as Daniel Webster Highway.

Though he served nearly three decades in Congress, the only significant piece of legislation Daniel Webster introduced resulted in prepaid postage stamps for the U.S. Post Office, eleven of which have borne his likeness, far more than any president. No doubt "Black Dan"—as some of his detractors called him—would be pleased to hear that he beat out so many U.S. presidents in that regard, an office he sought unsuccessfully on three occasions.

# MANCHESTER

*New Hampshire's largest* city also boasts the highest population (110,000) of any New England city north of Boston. Manchester owes its present robust health and long history to its location on the Amoskeag Falls in the Merrimack River, which made it an ideal site for all manner of manufacturing at the height of the Industrial Revolution. In 1810, the town's first cotton-spinning mill was built. Within a few years, that one mill became three. Then, in 1846, when it incorporated as a city, the largest cotton mill in the world opened: Mill No. 11 was 900 feet long, 103 feet wide, and housed 4,000 looms. In addition to millwork, a varied array of goods such as rifles, sewing machines, fire engines, shoes, locomotives, and cigars were manufactured in Manchester.

In 2009, *Forbes* magazine listed the "Queen City" as number one on its "America's 100 Cheapest Places to Live" list, and in 1998, *Money Magazine* called it the "number-one small city in the East." It is also famous as a center for shopping and entertainment, and is home to the Mall of New Hampshire, a 120-store, 1,000,000-square-foot

The Queen City Rules! City of Manchester: www.manchester nh.gov

Manchester-Boston Regional Airport: www .flymanchester .com

shopping destination, and the 10,000-seat Verizon Wireless Arena. World-renowned Currier Museum of Art's collection includes works by Picasso, Monet, and O'Keeffe. The century-old Palace Theatre hosts shows year-round, and the Millyard Museum offers historical exhibits. The Amoskeag Fishways Center lets visitors peek at river life via underwater windows, and Valley Cemetery, built in 1841, is a unique garden-style resting place. The city is home to a number of professional sports teams, including AAA baseball's New Hampshire Fisher Cats; the American Hockey League's Manchester Monarchs; the Manchester Wolves football team; and two roller-derby teams.

In recent years, the Manchester-Boston Regional Airport has been one of New England's go-to travel hubs. Used by most major airlines, it serves as a backup airport to Boston's Logan. The Queen City dining scene thrives at Café Momo, with Nepali dishes, and the Puritan Restaurant, since 1917, serves American and Greek food. And the Red Arrow Diner, open since 1922, is a twenty-four-hour joint that does what diners do best.

# NEW HAMPSHIRE STATE HOUSE

*In 1814, the competition* for the location of New Hampshire's capital city came down to three contending towns: Hopkinton, Salisbury, and Concord. Despite the fact that Salisbury offered a tempting $7,000 as an incentive, Concord won out. Being thrifty Yankees, the New Hampshirites in charge decided to use local granite (what else?) to erect a state house that was impressive, yet not so grand that it broke the bank. The prisoners at the nearby New Hampshire State Prison, who had built their own facility in 1812, were the logical choice for the cutting, shaping, and facing of the granite blocks. The structure's initial cost? A mere $82,000.

In 1857, it was determined that the state house was too small. Several years and $200,000 later, by 1866 it began to resemble the stalwart structure we all know today. This scenario came up again in 1903, and though the people of Manchester offered money (their second such offer over the years) to relocate the capitol to their fair city, the legislature voted to keep Concord as the capital.

*When in Concord, look for the gold dome! The State House Visitors Center is open year-round for tours, Monday through Friday, 8 a.m. to 4:30 p.m.; www.nh.gov*

THE NATION'S OLDEST STATE HOUSE IN WHICH THE LEGISLATURE STILL OCCUPIES ITS ORIGINAL CHAMBERS

1819     JUNE 2     1969

The state house was affixed with elevators, electricity, and vaults. In 1937, an annex was built, connecting to the state house via an underground passage.

Within the state house, the Hall of Flags boasts 107 New Hampshire battle flags from the Civil War through present-day conflicts. The walls of the senate chamber are lined with historic murals, while the 400-seat house chamber—the largest state legislative body in the United States—is lined with arched windows and portraits of past leaders.

The 2.6-acre grounds are enclosed by a granite fence, and statues on the grounds include Daniel Webster, General John Stark, John P. Hale, and New Hampshire's only U.S. president, Franklin Pierce (and the first born in the nineteenth century, in 1804, in a log cabin in Hillsborough).

Despite such a long history and seeming lack of space, New Hampshire can boast that, having first met there in 1819, theirs is the oldest state house in the United States in which the legislature still occupies its original chambers.

# MAPLE SYRUP

In mid-February, the frigid winter air in New Hampshire takes on a dry, sweet tang, a heady perfume that signals the onset of sugaring season. For the next six weeks, the state's hundred or so maple-syrup makers set to work producing approximately 90,000 gallons of the sweet stuff. Though it's roughly a tenth of what its western neighbor, Vermont, produces, New Hampshire's syrup makes up for the lower quantity with high quality, often winning blind taste tests.

Hundreds of years ago, native Algonquins sliced into the bark of maples to release the sweet sap of spring, which they called *sinzibuckwud,* or "drawn from trees." Today, high-tech methods of tapping trees involve plastic pipelines and reverse-osmosis systems, but one thing remains unchanged: Granite Staters are true maple aficionados, a good many of them dousing their daily cornflakes and oatmeal with the stuff, or frying their morning eggs and bacon in it.

Syrup produced early in the season is usually lighter amber in color, and as the season advances, the sap, and thus the syrup, becomes darker, but with a

*Mapley goodness awaits: New Hampshire Maple Producers Association (NHMPA): www.nhmaple producers.com*

*New Hampshire Maple Experience Museum: www.nhmaple experience.com*

*Mount Cube Sugar Farm: www.mtcube farm.com*

*Ben's Sugar Shack: www.bens-maple-syrup.com*

bolder, more "mapley" flavor. It comes in two grades, A and B, and in subgrades from light (also called "fancy") amber, medium amber, to dark amber; Grade B is even darker than dark amber. But these are not quality designations; rather, each grade is unique.

Every spring, to cap off New Hampshire's long and luscious maple season, more than sixty Granite State maple producers fling wide their sugarhouse doors and show visitors how sap (of which it takes forty gallons to produce just one gallon of syrup) becomes syrup. Some offer horse-dawn rides through their sugarbushes—the stands of maples they tap—and share that singular treat, sugar on snow.

Visitors who happen to miss the maple season can visit the New Hampshire Maple Experience at the historic Rocks Estate in Bethlehem. And numerous mom-and-pop shops sell all manner of New Hampshire–made maple products, such as lip-smacking maple relish, maple candy, maple fudge, maple salad dressing, maple ice cream, maple butter, maple mustard, and oh my yes . . . maple syrup!

# CANTERBURY SHAKER VILLAGE

The United Society of Believers in Christ's Second Appearing formed in 1747 in England. They were regarded by outsiders as "Shaking Quakers" because of their violent physical actions during services. In the late eighteenth century, leaders in the movement emigrated to the United States, and by 1840, they had 6,000 members in nineteen communities from Maine to Kentucky. Though today the last three Shakers in the world live at Maine's Sabbathday Lake Shaker Village, the legacy of the Shakers is in their historical village sites, in the quality of their construction techniques, and their sturdy, no-frills architecture and furniture, elegant examples of form following function.

And nowhere are these characteristics better exemplified than at the Canterbury Shaker Village and Museum, in Canterbury, New Hampshire, the most intact Shaker community in the United States. At the time of its founding in 1792, it was the seventh Shaker community, but would become one of the most prosperous, home to 300 community members who constructed 100 buildings and tended 3,000 acres of land. By the

*Families are most welcome at 288 Shaker Road, Canterbury; (603) 783-9511; www.shakers.org. The village is open daily from mid-May through October.*

1830s, the Canterbury Village Shakers were rich in land, buildings, cash, and livestock. In addition to marketing and selling their high-quality handmade goods, they also ministered to the poor and sick, and supported causes aimed at social good.

The Canterbury Village site lost its last member in 1992, and since then has operated solely as a museum. It is one of New Hampshire's top cultural attractions, and is run by Canterbury Shaker Village, Inc., a nonprofit organization established in 1969. It offers thousands of visitors each year as complete an education about Shakers and their way of life as it is possible to experience through archives of research materials, and exhibits of Shaker-made objects such as straw brooms, oval boxes, and furniture. Visitors are also invited to a series of special events throughout the year, such as meetinghouse concerts and candlelit Christmas strolls, plus tours of the twenty-five restored original Shaker buildings, and 694 acres of gardens, fields, forests, nature trails, and ponds—all protected from development through permanent conservation easements.

# CONCORD COACHES

*Abbot-Downing* Concord Coaches didn't invent stagecoaches, but it could be said that in 1827, it reinvented them, by making the basic design even better. The firm directly addressed passengers' most common complaint—that stagecoach rides were stiff, bone-shaking affairs. Abbot-Downing's solution? Leather-strap suspension made its Concord Coaches far more comfortable than any other coaches on the market—so comfy, in fact, that Mark Twain famously referred to the coach as a "cradle on wheels."

Soon, Abbot-Downing's customers advertised to the public that they used Concord Coaches exclusively. And so well-built were they that it was said Abbot-Downing coaches didn't break—they just wore out. For two decades the Abbot-Downing company enjoyed tremendous success. Then in 1847, the partners split. Abbot stayed put while Downing moved across the street. Each company did well on its own, and by 1865 the patriarchs had left their companies in the hands of their respective sons, who promptly ended the eighteen-year feud and rejoined forces, forming the Abbot-Downing Company.

**See why it's called a "cradle on wheels" at Six Gun City: www.sixguncity.com**

**The Abbot-Downing Historical Society: www.concordcoach.org**

And that's when things really kicked off: The opening of the West demanded reliable coach transport, and Abbot-Downing filled that need. The firm offered its most popular model in three sizes: six-, nine-, and twelve-passenger, and in three styles: City, Western, and Hotel. Basic models weighed 2,500 pounds, and bore an opening price of roughly $1,200 each. For years, more people rode westward in Concord Coaches than in any other conveyance.

But by the end of the century, with the advent of the Industrial Revolution, trains and automobiles made horse-drawn coaches all but unnecessary, and Abbot-Downing turned out its last stagecoach in 1899, after having built approximately 1,700. Today, 157 remain, 18 of them in New Hampshire. A number of fine examples are owned by the Abbot-Downing Historical Society and can be seen at its museum on the Hopkinton Fairgrounds in Contoocook. And Number 41, the oldest Concord Coach known to exist, built on November 29, 1846, makes its home, fittingly enough, at Six Gun City, the Wild West–themed amusement park, in Jefferson.

JEFFERSON HILL HOUSE.

S.T. CONNARY.

STAGE COACH
STRONG BOX

CONCORD COACH

The Spectacular Hotel Style Concord Coach is
the oldest known Concord Coach in existence.
It was built by the Abbot-Downing Co. of
Concord, N.H. and completed on Nov. 29, 1846.
During the 1800's it was used at the Jefferson Hill
House, Jefferson, N.H. Purchased in April, 1980 at
auction by S.G.C. at a cost of $58,000

# FROST HEAVES

*Frost heaves are* New Hampshire's ultra-abundant bumper (scraping) crop, one that never needs planting, but always comes up, without fail. Every March in New Hampshire, residents strap on their driving helmets and prepare themselves for their morning commutes. It's also the time of year when garage owners rub their hands together as if they were kindling fire, mischievous grins on their faces and their eyes glinting as they order extra shocks, struts, mufflers, and tires, and dust off their alignment machines. It's frost-heave season.

Scientifically, frost heaves are the result of repeated freezing and thawing of surfaces (most notably roads), which pushes and pulls rocks and dirt so that a street's surface can resemble a lumpy, bunched-up quilt. The bumps themselves can be fun to drive over, especially at higher-than-recommended rates of speed, and frequently result in unintentional flights of whoop-up fancy. Though the landing's the thing to watch out for, it can bring the teeth together hard, tongue be darned.

*Can't avoid 'em, might as well laugh about 'em: www.frostheaves.com*

The depressions, caused by sinkings instead of protrusions, aren't nearly as fun, causing cars to bottom out, sparks to shower, plastic parts to scrape, and hubcaps to pinwheel off into muddy culverts (another detriment of frost-heave season is that it roughly coincides with mud season). Of course, sometimes the bumps and bowls don't go away by the end of the season, in late April . . . or May.

Frost heaves aren't just relegated to the roads, however; as the earth yawns and stretches, working out the kinks after a long winter's nap, many folks wake to find cracks in their foundations, disjointed deck posts, and lumps in their driveways where head-size rocks had lingered unseen.

The only saving grace of frost-heave season is that it's one of the surest signs of spring. A costly one, to be sure, but New Hampshire residents know that if they can just ride it out, albeit a wee bit bruised and with a rattley car, they'll emerge into the warmth and promise of a greening spring in the White Mountain State. And next frost-heave season will be a lifetime away . . .

# MACDOWELL COLONY

In 1896, composer Edward Mac-Dowell and his pianist wife, Marian, bought an isolated farm in Peterborough, at which he might work without distraction. For a time, it proved to be just what he'd hoped. But in 1907, as he succumbed to dementia, Edward and his wife developed the farm into an artists' retreat so that other creative types might also benefit from the peaceful surroundings.

Today, the MacDowell Colony, the nation's oldest and most famous artists' retreat, sits on 450 acres of both wooded and open countryside where artists experience the gift of solitude and lack of distraction that can last from two weeks to two months. The mission of the colony remains simple: "To nurture the arts by offering creative individuals of the highest talent an inspiring environment in which they can produce enduring works of the imagination." Marian MacDowell famously remarked that this gift of time would " . . . prevent the non-writing of a great poem."

Open year-round since 1955, more than 250 filmmakers, writers, visual art-

*The home of creative inspiration— 6,000 artists can't be wrong: www.macdowell colony.org*

ists, composers, filmmakers, playwrights, interdisciplinary artists, and architects attend annually, roughly half of whom are repeat visitors, with twenty to thirty artists in residence at any one time. In 1962, the colony was designated a National Historic Landmark, and in 1997, the colony was awarded the National Medal of the Arts, the highest arts accolade bestowed by the U.S. government.

Few of the thirty-two comfortably appointed artists' studios are in sight of others. Composers' studios have pianos, wall space is ample in studios of visual artists, photography studios have darkrooms, and all studios are equipped with basic amenities. Picnic lunches are delivered midday, and at night, residents gather at communal spaces for dining, socializing, and sharing work.

Since its inception in 1907, more than 6,000 artists have attended the MacDowell Colony, earning more than sixty-five Pulitzer Prizes, a dozen MacArthur Foundation "Genius Awards," and numerous other prizes including Guggenheims, National Book Awards, Academy Awards, and GRAMMYs.

# MOUNT MONADNOCK

*In a bit of unusual* whimsy, Abenaki Indians were the ones to actually name this mountain—unusual because they rarely named anything that didn't hold some sort of distinction. So appropriate is the name *Monadnock,* which means "mountain that stands alone," that not only did whites uncharacteristically *not* change the name to suit their own desires, but geologists the world over have since come to use the word *monadnock* to describe similar formations, sitting as it does in bold and plain sight for all to see at 3,165 feet, approximately 1,000 feet higher than any other peak within 30 miles.

Better known as Mount Monadnock or Grand Monadnock, both Dublin and Jaffrey claim to be the mountain's hometown. The first recorded white to climb the peak was Captain Samuel Willard, who did so in 1725. Since then the centrally located pile has hosted hordes of hikers—and then some. Sixty-two miles northwest of Boston and 38 miles southwest of Concord, Monadnock is the most-climbed mountain in North America, with more than 125,000 people ascending it each

*Views await at Monadnock State Park: 116 Poole Road, Jaffrey; www.nhstateparks.org.*

year. In fact, it is only outdone globally by Mount Fujiyama in Japan, which hosts 200,000 climbers annually, and China's Mount Tai, which sees some two million.

One can make the climb to Monadnock's summit from any of six access points, and on more than 30 miles of trails. New England offers few climbs as rewarding, for once atop Mount Monadnock's broad rocky plateau, hikers will find on a clear day that they can see a wee bit of each of New England's six states—the only spot in New England where this is possible.

Mount Monadnock has been memorialized in operas, symphonies, waltzes, poems, paintings, fiction, and essays. In fact, it is said that Mount Monadnock is the most-written-about mountain in the United States. It would be an understatement to say that the mountain can become an obsession: Consider power hiker Larry Davis, who climbed to the peak on 2,850 consecutive days, and Garry Harrington, who in a single twenty-four-hour period climbed the mountain sixteen times. Obsessed? Maybe; but think of the views!

# STONYFIELD FARM

The top-selling organic yogurt (and the third-best-selling yogurt overall) in the United States grew from the humblest of cultures back in 1983, in Wilton, when Samuel Kaymen and Gary Hirshberg ran a small farming school. What began with a handful of Jersey cows and an urge to market their own product soon blossomed into a rising number of sales of their own yogurt line. Annual sales in that first year were a respectable $56,000.

As yogurt sales grew, the partners realized that their chances of making a positive difference in the lives of family farmers lay with their increasingly successful yogurt. As if to prove the point, by 1984, annual sales had increased to $138,000. Four years later, Stonyfield Farm moved 30 miles eastward to a custom-built facility in its current home of Londonderry. Annual yogurt sales reached $1,100,000 in 1988.

Today, Stonyfield's products include yogurt drinks, frozen yogurt, ice cream, Greek-style yogurt, soy yogurts, yogurt for babies, and plain old milk, all of it organic. Continuing its commitment to organic farming and sustainable

*It's all yogurt, all the time, at Stonyfield Farm Yogurt Works and Visitors Center: (603) 437-4040; www.stonyfield .com*

farming practices, Stonyfield purchases its milk from a cooperative network of family farmers in New England and the Midwest, and has helped to keep more than 200,000 acres of agricultural land free of the pesticides and chemicals often used in nonorganic farming practices.

Stonyfield Farm has stuck to its original 1983 mission—to be as sustainable as possible. The largest solar electric system in New Hampshire sits atop the roof of Stonyfield Farm's Londonderry plant. The company is active socially and environmentally, donating 10 percent of its annual profits to its "Profits for the Planet" program. It also uses the space on millions of yogurt-product lids each week to promote causes such as breast cancer awareness.

In 2001, Stonyfield Farm entered into a partnership with Groupe Danone, and although the French conglomerate owns 85 percent of Stonyfield Farm, Danone allows the New Hampshire–based company to operate as though it were still independently owned. After all, if it ain't broke . . . Stonyfield Farm's annual sales now top $360,000,000.

# THE OLD FARMER'S ALMANAC AND YANKEE MAGAZINE

From a most-humble beginning in 1935—with fourteen subscribers, printed on a press rescued from the bottom of the Connecticut River—*Yankee Magazine* was intended by its founder, Robb Sagendorph, to be "for Yankee readers, by Yankee writers, and about Yankeedom," his rough definition of a Yankee presumably as someone from (or in love with) New England. His emphasis on travel, the doings in the average Yankee household, and Yankee food, history, and agriculture all combined to accurately reflect the very essence of life in New England, a place at once mysterious and alluringly bucolic to people the world over.

In part to supplement his struggling publication, in 1939 Sagendorph purchased America's oldest continuously published periodical, *The Old Farmer's Almanac*. He became its eleventh editor since it began in 1792, and it would be the *Almanac* that would keep the company afloat during the lean years. Sagendorph also became well-known for his uncanny weather predictions, which employ an intricate blend of solar

The authority on all things New England: Yankee Publishing Inc., Dublin; www.Yankee Magazine.com; www.Almanac .com; www. Almanac4 Kids.com

activity, astronomical cycles, and weather patterns, all combined with a secret forecasting formula passed down through the centuries and still used today, and that the editors claim is 80 percent accurate.

Even during World War II's tight times, the *Almanac* was still published, and its popularity proved far-reaching. (A German spy was captured in New York City with a 1942 copy of the *Almanac* in his pocket.) It is published in four editions a year and distributed to more than four million readers. Its motto: "Useful, with a pleasant degree of humor."

Now edited by Judson Hale, Sagendorph's nephew, *Yankee* is still a respected voice on all things New England. It has a paid circulation of more than a half-million subscribers, with a readership exceeding two million, and employs seventy people. Still based in Dublin, New Hampshire, Yankee Publishing, Inc., continues to be a family-owned company, stone wall–solid, documenting the goings-on in New England (and predicting the national weather trends) as it has for more than seventy-five years.

Photo Essay
Easy
Best Ice Cream
in New England (p. 70)
From

Remembering
Christa McAuliffe (p. 14)
ow Co

Living Off
the Grid (p. 80)

YANKE

YANKE

NEW ENGLAND'S MAGAZINE

Class

Explo

Ne

THE FO

Our Apple Expert's
Favorite Recipes (p. 70)

YANK

NEW ENGLAND'S MAGAZINE

Top 10 Historic I

Co

Enjoy a Classic
Pumpkin Dessert (p.

8 Traditional
Toy Makers (p. 21) | Ho
Survive

YANKE

al
ENGLAND'S MAGAZINE

Everything under the Sun,
including the Moon

No.
CCXX

SUMMER

SPRING

THE

OLD
FARMER'S
2012
ALMANAC

BY
ROBERT B. THOMAS

THE ORIGINAL ROBERT B. THOMAS *Farmer's* ALMANAC, FOUNDED IN 1792

ALSO FEATURING ASTRONOMICAL TABLES, TIDES, HOLIDAYS, ECLIPSES, ETC.

AUTUMN

WINTER

HOLIDAYS

WEATHER FORECASTS
For 16 Regions of the United States

$6.95

ISBN: 978-1-57198-544-6

PLANTING TABLES, ZODIAC SECRETS

9 781571 985446

# NEW HAMPSHIRE MOTOR SPEEDWAY

*New Hampshire* Motor Speedway is the largest sports facility (seating-wise) in New England. The 1.058-mile oval speedway, built in 1990, sits on 1,100 acres just an hour north of Boston, in Loudon. Up to 105,491 shouting race fans jam the stands at top capacity, 93,521 of whom are packed into the grandstand, the rest filling 38 VIP suites.

And yet, all those motorsports aficionados also have other needs during long, hot race days, so there are 26 concession stands, 25 restrooms, 5 ATMs, 5 helipads, and 4 elevators. And those are just the outfield facilities. The infield, the holy grail for racing fans, includes a media center, four 26-bay enclosed garages, an inspection building, an ATM, the Smoke Shack barbecue grill, restrooms, a welding shop, and the 80-foot-tall scoreboard tower. Plus, race-crew access to the infield is provided via two 130-foot-long, 20-foot-diameter tunnels capable of accommodating tractor trailers. And all this is tended to by more than 1,500 employees.

In addition to the oval, used by stock cars, modified cars, and trucks,

Motor on over! 1122 Route 106 North, Loudon; Ticket Hotline: (603) 783-4931; www.nhms.com

there's a 1.6-mile road course for motorcycles, sports cars, karts, and more, as well as a quarter-mile mini oval. The speedway hosts a variety of NASCAR, IndyCar, and other events each year that are attended by more people than attend the NFL's Super Bowl.

When it officially opened on June 5, 1990, as New Hampshire International Speedway, it became the first superspeedway constructed in the United States since 1969. In its construction, more than 1.5 million cubic yards of earth were moved, 30,000 cubic yards of ledge were blasted, and more than 100,000 tons of asphalt were laid. The track's surface is a 5-inch-thick coat of asphalt, and the reinforced tunnels are a mere 3 feet beneath Turn 2.

The underground conduit that carries electricity and serves 300 phone lines is more than 20 miles long, there are 7 miles of water pipe, and 4 miles of steel cable reinforce the fence surrounding the oval. And this entire infrastructure ensures that on race days, the only thing fans see are those colorful cars whipping around that massive oval.

# HART'S TURKEY FARM RESTAURANT

*No one exemplifies* the old adage, "Do one thing and do it well," more than the Hart family, because they do turkey, and they do it *very* well. In fact, the word *gobble* takes on a whole new meaning when you pull up to Hart's Turkey Farm Restaurant in Meredith. It all started back in the late 1940s, when brothers Russ and Larry Hart and their wives left New Jersey for New Hampshire, in pursuit of an agricultural life. They sold their veggies, apples, chickens, turkey, and eggs from a delivery truck. By 1953, they had narrowed their product line down to turkeys, and the following year, they opened a twelve-seat eatery with an emphasis on "quality, service, and home-style cooking"—and a whole lotta turkey.

Since then, that amount has only increased. The family's flagship restaurant, in Meredith, overlooking Lake Winnipesaukee, has expanded from its dozen-seat status into a 500-seat behemoth that serves one ton of turkey, 1,000 pounds of fresh spuds, 4,000 din-

*When you're ready to talk turkey, visit Hart's at 233 Daniel Webster Highway, Junction of Routes 3 & 104, Meredith; (603) 279-6212; www .hartsturkey farm.com*

ner rolls, 40 gallons of gravy, and more than 100 pies—every day! Not only that, but practically everything on the menu is made on the premises, including whipped potatoes, rolls, and the turkeys, roasted fresh every day.

Add to that its lounge and bar, gift shop, ample parking (even for tour buses), a popular catering service capable of serving thousands at a single event, on-site or off-, and you have a genuine family empire founded on turkey dishes such as turkey pie, turkey meatloaf, turkey divan, turkey croquettes, jumbo turkey leg (from a 35-pound bird!). Or how about a heaping turkey plate (white, dark, or both) with potato or rice, vegetables, sliced apples, homemade rolls, corn bread, gravy, stuffing, and cranberry sauce?

And if, for some odd reason, there's a member of the family who's not a fan of turkey (egads!), Hart's serves up a full menu of beef, ham, pork, pasta, and seafood. But at Hart's, it always comes back to turkey, where, as they say, every day is Thanksgiving Day.

# HANCOCK VILLAGE

It is difficult to imagine a more quintessential New England village than Hancock. Settled in 1764, and founded in 1779, the town gets its name from the man whose bold flourish of a signature claimed so much visual real estate on the Declaration of Independence. John Hancock, the first Massachusetts governor and president of the Continental Congress, owned nearly 2,000 acres in town.

Every building on Hancock's Main Street is listed on the National Register of Historic Places, including Hancock Market, Fiddlehead's Cafe, a white-clapboard U.S. post office, the church, and the town green, complete with a gazebo that hosts weekly summer concerts, just across the way from the redbrick Vestry. Plus, the village is lined with quaint clapboard and brick homes, and the town's original schoolhouse.

Hancock is also home to Paul Revere's bell, #236, which chimes every hour on the hour, from its perch in the white-steepled belfry of the Meeting House. There is also a covered bridge, a tree-lined cemetery with weathered, hand-carved headstones

*Cute, quaint, quintessential: The Town of Hancock: www .hancocknh.org*

*The Hancock Inn: 33 Main Street, Hancock; (800) 525-1789; www .hancockinn.com*

(bucolic in the daytime and positively spooky on a late-fall evening!), stone walls, and dirt lanes. In summer, swimming and boating is the order of the day at Norway Pond, the beach of which is but a short walk from the village, and in winter it's *the* place to ice-skate. And five miles from the village, the Harris Center nature preserve offers a number of relaxing walking trails.

One of the most impressive sites in the town is the Hancock Inn, the oldest New Hampshire inn still in operation, and one of the oldest inns in New England. It opened its doors to guests for the first time in 1789, and has retained all of its eighteenth-century historic charm and world-class, award-winning dining.

But Hancock isn't all gravel lanes and quaint scenes. It's also home to the Very Long Baseline Radio Telescope, a deep-space telescope that's one of seven in the continental United States. This big space ear, which listens for radio particles from galaxies millions of light years away, is operated via remote control by staff in New Mexico.

# ROBERT FROST

*Robert Frost spent* many of his formative years in New Hampshire, so it is with good cause that the state lays claim to being Frost's favorite place—and he the state's favorite poetical son. So fond was Frost of the Granite State, in fact, that he owned two different New Hampshire farms.

Frost is most associated with the white clapboard structure of the Robert Frost Farm in Derry. The farm belonged to his grandfather, who left it to him along with an annuity on his death in 1901. Frost and his wife lived there for a decade. Although he had intended to farm the place, his heart wasn't in it. Locals thought he was lazy, yet while there, he composed the poems that made up his first two books, *A Boy's Will* and *North of Boston*. He would go on to win the Pulitzer Prize for literature an unprecedented four times, and though he sold the Derry farm in 1911, it is arguably his time there that most influenced his greatest work.

Beginning in 1974, under the supervision of Frost's daughter,

*Robert Frost Farm: 122 Rockingham Road (Route 28), Derry; (603) 432-3091; www.robertfrostfarm.org*

*The Frost Place: 158 Ridge Road, Franconia; (603) 823-5510; frost@frostplace.org; www.frostplace.org*

Lesley Frost Ballantine, the Robert Frost Farm was restored to the condition it was in when the Frosts were in residence. Today, the house, barn, and grounds—47.5 acres laced with walking trails free and open to the public—are a New Hampshire State Park. A nominal admission fee to the house museum helps maintain the homestead.

Frost's other New Hampshire home, "The Frost Place" in Franconia, was owned by Frost and his wife from 1915 to 1920. Today it, too, is a lovingly maintained house museum, open to the public. In addition to hosting a poet-in-residence, it is home to a collection of signed first editions of Frost's work, and a series of walking trails.

The long tradition of bards finding inspiration among New Hampshire's rolling farmland and granite hills is carried on by many poets, among them Maxine Kumin, U.S. Poet Laureate (1981–82), and Donald Hall, U.S. Poet Laureate (2006–07), whose own family has long roots in New Hampshire.

# CASTLE IN THE CLOUDS

*In 1914, in the midst* of one of America's most amazing rags-to-riches-to-rags stories, newly married multimillionaire shoe manufacturer Thomas Gustave Plant retired at age fifty-one to his custom-built castle, which he dubbed "Lucknow." As the hub of his 6,300-acre estate, Plant's dream home is a stunning abode unparalleled in construction, style, and setting, overlooking Lake Winnipesaukee and the Ossipee Mountain range.

This stunning, sixteen-room, 5,500-acre estate took four years to complete, and employed 2,000 people who worked on it continuously. It was built of steel girders and heavy oak timbers faced with stonework that took on the blend-into-nature look of the Arts and Crafts movement. The home was the first in the region to be fitted with electricity. Lucknow also sported an intercom system, central vacuum, hand-painted glasswork, Tiffany glass skylights, "needle" showers that sprayed from multiple angles, and a secret room where Plant could do a bit of reading. And for the canine companions? A three-bay doghouse.

*Take in the stunning views and sumptuous surroundings at Castle in the Clouds, Route 171, 455 Old Mountain Road, Moultonborough; (603) 476-5900; www.castleinthe clouds.org*

Plant's great wealth (roughly $1 billion today) soon evaporated after a series of failed investments. He struggled to maintain his holdings through the Great Depression, and the Plants managed to hang on until 1941, when Tom Plant died. The estate was sold, and his wife went to live with her family in Illinois.

Lucknow exists today in near-new condition because subsequent owners never modernized anything. In fact, it retains nearly all of its period furnishings and excellent plasterwork. The view from Lucknow, now more commonly known as Castle in the Clouds, impresses thousands of visitors each year. After a tour of the grounds and home, they can partake of fine dining at the lauded Carriage House Cafe and Patio, shop at the Castle Gift Shop, tour the Art Gallery, and even go horseback riding. Lucknow also hosts a number of weddings and other private functions. Today, the Castle Preservation Society maintains the buildings, and the Lakes Region Conservation Trust manages the 5,245-acre estate, including 28 miles of walking paths, a stunning forest, a waterfall, and Shannon Pond, which is stocked with fat, happy trout.

# LACONIA MOTORCYCLE WEEK

*If you're into motorcycles* and someone mentions "Laconia" to you, anywhere in the world, you know just what they're talking about—none other than Laconia Motorcycle Week, the oldest continuous motorcycle event in the United States. Originating way back in 1916 with the Gypsy Tour, 2012 marks its eighty-ninth year. The nine-day rally attracts riders and aficionados from all over the globe in June each year to Weirs Beach, in Laconia, on the shores of Lake Winnipesaukee. Always wrapping up on Father's Day, its attendance peaked in 2004 with 375,000 bikers, but still hit a respectable 188,000 in 2010.

In the 1980s, attendance dwindled due to increased rowdiness, until it became a three-day event. This was not wholly unexpected; when tens of thousands of hard-core bikers and scantily clad biker chicks are packed into a relatively small place, there's bound to be trouble, and the rally is no stranger to its share of riots, bar fights, drag racing, and rough play. Eventually, in the 1990s, in an effort to increase tourist traffic, established

*Rev it up and roll on in! www.laconiamcweek.com*

motorcycle groups and local businesses came together to form the Laconia Motorcycle Rally and Race Association. It is charged with organizing and scheduling events throughout the rally, marketing the event nationwide, and lining up vendors. Nowadays, local merchants can't help but smile when June rolls around and the throaty roar of Harleys, Hondas, and Indians rolls its way into town.

So what do lots and lots of motorcycle aficionados do for more than a week in Laconia? There's lots of live music, T-shirt contests (some wet, some wild), perhaps a wee bit of imbibing of tasty brews. But for many folks, it's an annual opportunity to meet with fellow motorcycle nuts they haven't seen in a year. The week is filled with charity rides, plus the "Ride to the Sky" event to the top of Mount Washington. But even as the week idles down, it's not over with, because Father's Day roars to life in nearby Loudon, with the longest-running motorcycle race in the United States, the Loudon Classic, held at the New Hampshire Motor Speedway.

# LAKE WINNIPESAUKEE

*Rarely has a lake's name* been so fun to pronounce: *Win-ni-pe-sau-kee* means "Beautiful water of the high place," according to the Pemigewasset Indians, and is located in the heart of New Hampshire's summer playground region. Winnipesaukee is the largest lake in New Hampshire, the third largest in New England (behind Vermont's Champlain and Maine's Moosehead), and, at 72 square miles (that's 45,952 acres), it's the fifth-largest inland lake in the United States. It's 28 miles long, 15 miles wide at its widest point, 180 feet deep at its deepest spot, and it sports 365-plus islands—244 of which are habitable.

Since 1887, the annual Ice-Out Contest is determined by the date the cruise ship *Mount Washington* is able to trek to four spots safely. The earliest ice-out happened on March 24, 2010, the latest, on May 12, 1888. The date also signifies the end of winter in the state (though residents may chuckle at that as they look out their windows and see snowdrifts).

The lake offers every form of year-round distraction. In winter, ice-

So much to see and do!
Lake Winnipesaukee Home Page:
www.winnipesaukee.com

Lake Winnipesaukee Museum:
www.lwhs.us

M/S Mount Washington:
www.cruisenh.com

Lakes Region information:
www.lakewinnipesaukee.net

boating, skating, snowmobiling, and ice-fishing rule the day. And in summer there's waterskiing, boating, and fishing for salmon, lake trout, and bass—or lounging on fine-sand Weirs Beach, the lake's most popular strand, offering fried foods and cotton candy, muscle boys and bikini girls, suntan oil and baitfish . . .

A long succession of steamships have roamed the lake over the years, but the original *Mount Washington* outlasted them all, ferrying passengers for sixty-seven years, from her launch in 1872 to a December day in 1939, when fire razed the Weirs Beach train station and with it, the grand old steamship, which had been tied to the dock. A replacement, rechristened the *Mount Washington II* in honor of her predecessor, launched on August 12, 1940. The 230-foot-long vessel is still plying the waters of Lake Winnipesaukee, along with smaller sister vessels, among them the oldest floating post office in the United States, the mail boat *Sophie C.*, providing a summer mail service on the lake that began in 1892.

# DARTMOUTH COLLEGE

*World-famous* Dartmouth College, the ninth-oldest college in the United States, was founded in 1769 by Congregational minister Eleazar Wheelock, and eventually became the northernmost of the nation's highly regarded "Ivy League" schools. It is named for William Legge, Second Earl of Dartmouth, and one of Wheelock's early supporters.

Dartmouth is a financially healthy school, enjoying an endowment of $3.4 billion. It owns a whopping 31,869 acres worth roughly $434 million, making it the largest private landowner in Hanover, a Connecticut River border town of 11,000 residents.

Currently Dartmouth employs 995 academics who earn among the highest salaries of educators at US institutions of higher learning. The school enrolls 4,200 undergraduate students and 1,800 graduate students. It offers nineteen graduate programs, including the nation's fourth-oldest medical program (dating from 1797) and the first professional school of engineering in the United States. Athletics are also important to this NCAA Division I school, with thirty-four varsity teams playing a variety of sports.

*Northernmost of the Ivy Leagues: Dartmouth College, Hanover; (603) 646-1110; www.dartmouth .edu*

Despite its charter's specification that it be a school in large part for the education of "Youth of Indian Tribes," only 19 Native Americans graduated from Dartmouth in its first two centuries. However, since the 1970s, the school has increased Native American enrollment, and more than 700 Native American students have graduated from Dartmouth (a higher figure than all other seven Ivy League schools combined).

Famous New Hampshire son Daniel Webster was himself an 1801 graduate of the Big D's hallowed halls, and there are more than 60,000 living Dartmouth alumni worldwide. Over its 240-plus-year history, Dartmouth has graduated numerous high-profile folks, among them Nelson A. Rockefeller, Robert Reich, C. Everett Koop, Charles A. Pillsbury, and Fred Rogers.

Theodor Geisel graduated from Dartmouth in 1925, and while there he first used his now-famous pseudonym of Dr. Seuss. And Dartmouth is purported to be the inspiration for the seminal frat-house film *Animal House*, as one of its writers once studied at Dartmouth. Food fight, anyone?

# OLD MAN OF THE MOUNTAIN

Since 1805, when surveyors working in Franconia Notch saw what has alternately been called the Great Stone Face, the Profile, or, most popularly, the Old Man of the Mountain, Granite Staters have long felt a deep bond with that distant, lordly gaze symbolizing the inherent independence and defiance associated with New Hampshire and its denizens.

In 1850, famed New Hampshire native son Daniel Webster wrote of the significance of the Old Man: "Men hang out their signs indicative of their respective trades; shoe makers hang out a gigantic shoe; jewelers a monster watch; and the dentist hangs out a gold tooth; but up in the Mountain of New Hampshire, God Almighty has hung out a sign to show that there He makes men."

The Old Man was adopted in 1945 as part of the state's official emblem. Since then he has graced the state license plate, postage stamps, quarters, road signs, businesses, and T-shirts. Countless travelers zipping along Route 93, north and south, have craned their necks for a quick glimpse

*He may be gone, but the legend lives on: There are two viewing areas on I-93 in Franconia Notch State Park: A pull-off on the northbound side, and southbound, take Exit 34B and follow signs; www.nh.gov/visitors/oldman.htm*

of the reassuring profile.

But the beginnings of trouble were noticed in the 1920s, when cracks, caused by thawing and freezing, appeared in the Old Man's forehead. These were secured with chains, but by the late 1950s, the fissures had grown worse. Twenty tons of cement, steel rods, chains, and cables were implemented, and each summer brought more refurbishment efforts. Then, without warning, between midnight and 2 a.m. on May 3, 2003, the Old Man of the Mountain gave up the ghost. The stony formation—40 feet tall and 25 feet wide, perched 1,200 feet above Profile Lake, named for the Old Man—collapsed to rubble, alone and unseen.

In June 2010, the first official phase was unveiled of the Old Man of the Mountain Memorial, a sculptural installation along Interstate 93 of granite obelisks that will once again form the Old Man's profile. Viewers can follow the Old Man's example and gaze on the natural wonder that is New Hampshire's bold wilderness; after all, it seemed to be his favorite pastime, for far longer than we know.

# FRANCONIA NOTCH

*Franconia Notch* is a pass in the White Mountains of singular beauty, home to Franconia Notch State Park, a parkland that must be seen—and hiked—to be believed. Extending 8 miles from Flume Gorge, in Lincoln, at the southern end, to Echo Lake at the northern terminus, the Notch is a major corridor northward through the mountains. A thirty-year road-works project was completed in 1988 that expanded I-93, including the 12-mile Franconia Notch Parkway, through the heart of the Notch, affording easier passage of ample year-round commercial and tourist traffic.

The state-owned Cannon Mountain ski resort (so named for a cannon-shaped rock formation at the summit) is famous for its fifty-five challenging trails and its passenger tram, in operation since 1938. Seven million year-round passengers have taken the eight-minute ride in one of two cable cars to the top of the 4,200-foot peak. From the top, visitors can see New Hampshire, Maine, Vermont, Canada, and New York. Back at the base, the New England Ski Museum gets visitors fired up for another run at the slopes.

*For those who love the outdoors, Franconia Notch is a year-round treat: www.nhstateparks.org*

Visitors can enjoy classic fly-fishing at Profile Lake, headwaters of the Pemigewasset River, and picnicking along the shore is encouraged. Just above the lake sits the broad, 1,950-foot cliff that, until May 3, 2003, was home to the Old Man of the Mountain. Swimming at nearby Echo Lake is welcome after a hike on one of the many local trails, including the famed Appalachian Trail. And the Franconia Notch Bike Path traverses the entire length of the Notch.

At the base of a waterfall in the Pemigewasset River, a 20-foot-wide granite pothole known as the Basin, formed through fifteen millennia of pounding water and rock, sits just above the Old Man's Foot, another distinctive rock. The Notch is also home to the Flume Gorge and Visitor Center, in Lincoln, at the southern end.

The weather in the Notch can be unforgiving in winter, but visitors to any of New Hampshire's rugged mountain notches, among them Dixville and Crawford, shouldn't worry—unless they happen to become stranded during a February snowstorm . . .

# NORTH CONWAY

*Nestled smack-dab* in the middle of a year-round resort region—namely the nearly 800,000 acres of White Mountain National Forest—it would be difficult to find a more appropriate setting for North Conway, the town that calls itself the "birthplace of American skiing." Opportunities for outdoor adventure close by the tony town are unlimited, from hiking and biking to skiing and snowboarding. And all manner of accommodation awaits, from rustic campgrounds to the Eastern Slope Inn (listed on the National Register of Historic Places) to the North Conway Grand, top choice for shoppers.

The village of North Conway, the largest within the five-village cluster that make up the town of Conway, is famous for its outlet shopping—in which manufacturers sell their goods directly to the public at "discounted" prices. The popularity of such shopping in New Hampshire is strongly influenced by the fact that there's no sales tax, a detail that does not go unannounced by the local chamber of commerce.

In 1988, the Settlers' Green Outlet Village was built in North Conway,

*Shop 'til you drop—and then go skiing! Settlers' Green Outlet Village: www.settlersgreen.com*

*Cranmore Mountain Resort: www.cranmore.com*

*North Conway Grand Hotel: www.northconwaygrand.com*

*Eastern Slope Inn: www.easternslopeinn.com*

*North Conway 5 and 10: www.northconway5and10.com*

*Conway Scenic Railroad: www.conwayscenic.com*

and since then, more than sixty outlet shops in that mall alone have blossomed, including Eddie Bauer, J. Crew, Levis, Sunglass Hut, Lids, Coach, Talbots, Toys Я Us, Brookstone, Nike, and more. But North Conway is also home to numerous independent outlets, including L.L. Bean and Orvis.

But not all of North Conway's shops are new: The North Conway 5-and-10-Cent Store is the town's oldest continually operating retail space (since 1815). Also eminently historic, the Conway Scenic Railroad, with its restored 1874 Victorian station, makes its home at the historic North Conway Depot and Railroad Yard. Cranmore Mountain Resort is one of the state's most popular ski areas, and Tuckerman Ravine, on the southeastern side of Mount Washington, is the birthplace of today's extreme-skiing craze.

Yet no matter how much fun folks have on the slopes, the hiking trails, or nearby rivers, they all head back to the hundreds of outlet stores in North Conway for a bit of relaxing retail therapy. And North Conway is only too glad to be of service.

# LEAGUE OF NEW HAMPSHIRE CRAFTSMEN

The League of New Hampshire Craftsmen was established in 1932 during the Great Depression as a way to instigate an income for the state's cash-strapped crafters. The following year, the League's first annual Craft Fair was held in the Crawford House barn in Crawford Notch. Though it only generated $2,698, it exceeded the participants' expectations—so much so that they decided to make it an annual event. It has grown every year since in size, participation, attendance, and earnings, and settled on its current home in 1964, with future expansion in mind, at Mount Sunapee Resort.

Today, it is the oldest craft fair in the nation, with 2012 marking its seventy-ninth year. The nine-day August event hosts 35,000-plus visitors who purchase more than $2 million worth of crafts made exclusively by league members. It always runs on the first Saturday in August, rain or shine, from 10 a.m. to 5 p.m., and offers attendees more than 200 individual craft booths, a sculpture garden, boutiques, and more.

The League supports its thriving

**League of New Hampshire Craftsmen:
49 South Main Street, Suite 100, Concord; (603) 224-3375;
www.nhcrafts.org**

educational component at The Craft Center, in Concord, where it offers workshops, demonstrations, and master classes for craft professionals and amateurs of all ages and skill levels, and in such mediums as clay, fiber, glass, metal, and woodworking.

Not just anyone can join the League, though. Since it's a juried guild, only work approved by the League's rigorous standards program may be sold through its galleries, as well as at the annual fair and other League-sponsored events and venues. Each of its retail galleries offers extensive collections of traditional and contemporary fine crafts, with stunning displays of spun and blown glass, woodworking, claywork, fine jewelry, ornaments, basket making, fine furniture, calligraphy, fiberwork, leatherwork, metalwork, paper, and printmaking.

A visit to one of its eight statewide retail galleries, including its newest guild store on Main Street, in Concord, is the best way to take in all that the League of New Hampshire Craftsmen offers. Better yet, the curious can attend the annual Craftsmen's Fair in August. See you there!

# THE WHITE MOUNTAINS

*The highest mountain* chain in the Northeast is also the most rugged, with a series of ragged notches, sheer cliffs, and wind-filled bowls that intimidate the timid and tempt the adventurous. The White Mountains allegedly earned their name from early settlers, who, while still at sea, spied the far-off, snowcapped peaks. The Whites are anything but white for much of the year (certain rocky and snow-inclined peaks excluded). They bud green in the spring, fill out through the summer into a deeper shade of jade, and in autumn they are dazzling in their rustic splendor—reds, oranges, golds, the hues visually stunning.

Unlike the Green Mountain Chain in neighboring Vermont, which is contained wholly within that state, the White Mountains, composed of a series of smaller ranges, only occupy about a quarter of New Hampshire's real estate, from Piermont in the south to Cushman in the north, before breaching the border of its eastern neighbor, Maine. But the biggest, boldest part of the White Mountain range is ensconced within the Granite State's borders: Mount

*Always there, majestic, ready, and waiting: www.visitwhite mountains.com*

Washington and the series of raw, awesome declivities known as the Notches, twenty-six of which are in the White Mountains.

The range is also home to the first national forest east of the Mississippi, the White Mountain National Forest, established in 1918. Much of its 784,505 acres can be enjoyed through a variety of driving loops, hiking routes, and ski areas. This region includes two of the state's northernmost counties, Coos and Grafton, as well as several state parks including Mount Washington, Franconia Notch, Crawford Notch, Moose Brook, Pinkham Notch Scenic Area, and the ever-scenic Kancamagus Highway.

The Appalachian Trail runs west to east through the Whites, and the White Mountain National Forest is home to the "Four-Thousand Footers," a series of forty-eight peaks that rise to at least that height. Popular with peak-baggers (hikers who conquer lists of such lofty summits), they range from the shortest, Tecumseh, at 4,003 feet, to the tallest, Mount Washington, at 6,288 feet. Not for the faint of heart, but definitely for the adventurous.

# CLARK'S TRADING POST

One of the Granite State's few surviving 1920s roadside attractions, Clark's Trading Post continues to be a must-stop spot for families vacationing in New Hampshire's White Mountains. Since 1928, visitors to the famous, family-run, homespun amusement park have been educated as well as entertained. As proof, there are five separate museums at Clark's, housing everything from antique autos, fire engines, and train locomotives to all manner of Americana, from guns and typewriters to a rare (stuffed) two-headed calf.

Then there are the nifty gift shops, the photo parlor, the candle shop, the maple cabin, the ice-cream saloon, the pizza parlor, a world-class circus acrobatics act, the topsy-turvy house, the blaster boats—think bumper cars combined with high-powered squirt guns—the climbing tower, and the world's first Segway park (those funky balancing scooters just got even more fun).

Another Clark's high point is the thirty-minute, 2.5-mile trip on the

*Trains, museums, rides, bears, and a wild man . . . oh my! All that and more at 110 Daniel Webster Highway, Lincoln; (603) 745-8913; www.clarks tradingpost.com*

White Mountain Central Railroad's wood-burning, steam-powered locomotive train. It crosses the Pemigewasset River via the 1904 covered bridge and into the domain of the howling Wolfman, who chases the train in his jalopy, threatens riders, and shakes his mountain-man fists while train-riding children shout right back at him.

As great as all these attractions are, it's the Bear Show that's the real reason to visit—and revisit—Clark's. The family started with its first bear way back in 1931, as a way to tempt more tourists to stop. By 1949, the founders' sons, Edward and Murray, began training the expanding Clark's bear population for complex show work. Today, the world-famous half-hour Bear Show, running up to three times per day, from May through October, is still overseen and conducted by Clark family members. The unmuzzled and unleashed—and highly intelligent—Clark's bears play basketball, ride scooters, balance on balls, and more. Educational? Yep—and a whole lot of fun for the family, too.

# PUMPKINS

Thought to have originated in Central America in 5,500 BC, the thick-fleshed fruits (not vegetables!) were favored by New England's natives, who relied upon them as dietary staples, and even used strips from the dried fruit to weave with. Taught of the pumpkin's many wonders by Native Americans, European colonists soon figured out their own ways to prepare the curious fruit, filling hollowed pumpkins with milk, honey, and spices to make an early pie-like dish.

For such historic significance, and because there seem to be more pumpkins grown in the state than ever, the pumpkin was selected on July 5, 2006, by the New Hampshire legislature as the official state fruit. A sound choice, as the ubiquitous melon is available statewide from late summer through late fall at roadside stands, mom-and-pop markets, and pick-your-own pumpkin patches. The fruits come in all shapes, sizes, and colors, perfect for carving funky faces, while others are grown specifically for baking tasty treats for the upcoming holiday season.

*Pumpkins abound in New Hampshire:*
*Milford Pumpkin Festival:*
*www.milford pumpkinfestival .org*

*Keene Pumpkin Festival:*
*www.pumpkin festival.com*

*New Hampshire Giant Pumpkin Growers Association:*
*www.nhgpga.org*

*Giant Pumpkin Weigh-In & Regatta: Goffstown Village; www.goffstown mainstreet.org*

The New Hampshire Giant Pumpkin Growers Association holds an annul Giant Pumpkin Weigh-Off and Regatta each year in Goffstown Village in mid-October. The great gourds exceed 1,500 pounds and require forklifts to move them. The massive pumpkins also make interesting watercraft as, no matter how large they get, the brutes are naturally buoyant. Jackson hosts its twenty-fifth annual Return of the Pumpkin People displays throughout town for the month of October. And Milford's Pumpkin Festival, which turns twenty-three in 2012, is a three-day family event in early October with scarecrows, a giant pumpkin contest, a pumpkin catapult, and more.

Every October since 1992, the city of Keene works to break the world record for the most jack-o'-lanterns in one place at one time. From 1,628 in its inaugural year, the event broke the record seven more times, topping out at an amazing 29,762 glowing jacks in 2009 (sadly, 366 shy of Boston's record). But loss is not part of the Granite State lexicon, especially where its official state fruit is concerned . . .

# MOUNT WASHINGTON

*Even if most folks* didn't know that at 6,288 feet, Mount Washington is the highest peak in the Northeast, they would still gaze in awe at the mighty mountain. Despite the fact that local Indians called the mountain *Agiocochook,* the "Home of the Great Spirit," in 1642 a man named Darby Field climbed it, becoming the first white to reach the summit. In 1784, a party of geologists named the mountain; then, in 1819, the Crawford Path, leading from Crawford Notch to the summit, was established. Still in use today, it is considered the oldest mountain hiking trail in the United States.

But Mount Washington is perhaps best known for the distinction of being home to the world's worst weather, as recorded by the Mount Washington Observatory on the afternoon of April 12, 1934. Scientists in this collection of wind-battered structures (that are literally chained to the rock) recorded the highest wind speed in the world, a bold gust measured at 231 miles per hour. The summit receives an annual average of 110 days with winds exceeding hurricane force, most notably from

*Come on up, the view's amazing . . . Mount Washington Observatory: www.mount washington.org*

*Mount Washington Auto Road: www.mt washingtonauto road.com*

November through April. Early weather observations at the summit began in 1870, with an unofficial record low of -59°F recorded in 1871, a windchill record of -103°F recorded in January 2004, and an annual snowfall average of 311 inches.

Located in Sargent's Purchase, Coos County, all but 59 acres of the massive mountain is located within the White Mountain National Forest; the remaining bit—which includes the famous peak—is considered Mount Washington State Park. In the 1850s, two hotels were constructed at the peak, and a winding coach road later known as the Mount Washington Auto Road was built. In 1869, the world-famous Mount Washington Cog Railway began ferrying folks to the summit.

The Auto Road, which celebrated its 150th anniversary in 2011, regularly hosts competitive events for runners, bicyclists, and auto enthusiasts. But most visitors arrive in summer and drive the family car to the top, where they qualify for one of those ubiquitous bumper stickers that read THIS CAR CLIMBED MOUNT WASHINGTON.

# MOUNT WASHINGTON COG RAILWAY

*While hiking* Mount Washington one day in 1857, Sylvester Marsh, of Campton, thought that a railway might be just the thing to get people from the bottom to the top. Fortunately for him, everyone—including the state legislature—thought he was nuts. So naturally, they decided to let him proceed. It helped that he was willing to pony up $5,000 of his own money to get the train rolling. Marsh persisted, built a hotel at the base in anticipation of the hordes of travelers he expected, and attracted investors based on a prototype engine and short run of track. His gamble paid off, and by 1869, the Cog's unique 3-mile-long rail-and-rack tracks reached the summit of Mount Washington, and has been in operation ever since.

Until recently, the train operated on a ratcheting mechanism involving a toothed cogwheel that clicked into place on a rack between the rails as the locomotive pushes from behind a single passenger car. The new mechanism incorporates clutches and disc brakes, and is considered even safer. The Mount Washington Cog Railway is the

*Do the Cog! On the Base Road, 6 miles off Route 302; Bretton Woods; (800) 922-8825; www .thecog.com*

world's first mountain-climbing cog railway, and has the steepest grade of any railroad in the world.

The trains run from late April through early December, and round-trips take about three hours. Trains depart from the Marshfield Base Station, with its restaurant, gift shop, and museum, and passengers spend one hour going up, one hour at the summit, and one hour heading back down. The railway has ferried more than five million people to and from the summit since it began operations in 1869. In 1941, the railway was made even more efficient when side tracks and switching systems were instituted, allowing for multiple cars to operate simultaneously.

Over the years, the engines have run on wood, coal, diesel, and now, in an effort to reduce what is affectionately called "Cog Smog," the fleet is being converted to a biodiesel mix. This produces less exhaust and runs more efficiently, though a coal-fired locomotive still makes an early-day run for the steam-power buffs in the crowd. After all, this is a historic railroad.

# GRAND HOTELS

*Only four true* Grand Hotels remain in New Hampshire, the last shining examples of a statewide collection that once numbered four hundred.

The Wentworth by the Sea (opposite, bottom right), in New Castle, built in 1874, was scheduled for a date with the wrecking ball in 1982 when the non-profit Friends of the Wentworth attracted a consortium to buy her. In 2003, after a $30 million investment, it reopened as the Wentworth by the Sea Hotel and Spa. One century earlier it hosted the negotiations that ended the Russo-Japanese War. Today, it once again hosts dignitaries, with 161 rooms, a grand ballroom, and an 8,500-square-foot spa.

When it opened on July 28, 1902, with a staff of 350, The Mount Washington Hotel (opposite, top right) boasted a power plant, a private telephone system, and a post office. Fifty trains a day arrived, filled with wealthy summer guests. In 1944, the hotel hosted the conference at which the World Bank and International Monetary Fund were established. In 1991, New Hampshire businessmen purchased the hotel, its two golf courses, and Bretton

*Step back in time (with modern conveniences): Wentworth by the Sea Hotel and Spa: www.wentworth.com*

*Mount Washington Hotel: www.brettonwoods.com*

*Mountain View Grand: www.mountainviewgrand.com*

*The Balsams: www.thebalsams.com*

Woods Ski Area, and since 1999 it has been a year-round luxury resort.

In 1865, the Dodge family took in its first boarders. Renamed the Mountain View House, by 1912 it could accommodate 200 guests. In 1986, the oldest resort in the United States to be owned and operated by the same family finally closed its doors. But in 2002, a young entrepreneur reopened the resort after a $20-million renovation. Sited on 1,700 wooded acres in the White Mountains, The Mountain View Grand (opposite, top left) is known for its fine dining and incredible views of fifty-seven peaks.

In 1895, Philadelphia industrialist Henry S. Hale bought the twenty-five-room summer inn, The Dix House. He renamed it The Balsams (opposite, bottom left) and expanded its offerings, until, by 1918, it reached its current capacity of 400 rooms. Famed for its striking setting amid 8,000 acres, guests enjoy golfing, skiing, canoeing, and fishing. The Balsams is renowned for its four-star dining room, and holds high status as the location of tiny Dixville Notch's first-in-the-nation presidential primary voting.

# KANCAMAGUS HIGHWAY

*If you're an inveterate* leaf-peeper, odds are you've traveled the 26.5-mile-long leg of New Hampshire Route 112, itself a 56-mile-long state highway that runs in the northern climes of the state, connecting Bath with Conway, from west to east. "The Kanc," as it's known locally, is actually the eastern half of Route 112. It's considered by many to be the best fall foliage trip anywhere in the United States, and is officially designated as an American Scenic Byway by the U.S. Department of Transportation. If you're from New Hampshire, you'll be excused for claiming it as one of the prettiest drives in the world. And if you're not from New Hampshire, once you've driven it during peak foliage season, you'll understand that such hometown hubris is well-founded.

A surefire way to reveal one's status as an out-of-stater is to pronounce it "Kanca-MANG-us," a definite no-no. Correctly pronounced "Kanca-MAH-gus," Kancamagus, which means "Fearless One," is named for the grandson of Passaconaway, a revered Indian leader who, in 1627, was responsible for uniting seventeen tribes from New England,

*From Conway, take Route 16 to 112 west, follow signs; from Lincoln, take Route 112 east, follow signs . . . and enjoy!*

which ultimately resulted in the Penacook Confederacy.

Opened in 1959, the Kancamagus Highway connects two previously dead-end roads, and links Conway's Route 16 with Interstate 93 in Lincoln. The drive, traveling east to west, Conway to Lincoln (or vice-versa), winds along the Swift River valley before summiting 2,855-foot Kancamagus Pass, then dips back down along the Pemigewasset River's east branch to Lincoln. The route is punctuated with a number of scenic pull-offs ideal for snapping pictures. It's a refreshing drive in part because it's uncluttered with billboards, service stations, and motels. Such amenities are plentiful in the towns bookending this scenic stretch, but travelers do have their choice between six campgrounds and a network of hiking trails along Route 112.

Other sights throughout the drive include Lower Falls and Rocky Gorge on Swift River, a covered bridge in Albany, and the historic Russell Colbath House, now operated by the U.S. Forest Service as a public information center. The road is open year-round—even in the winter. And it's a beautiful trip then, too.

# SQUAMSCOT OLD-FASHIONED BEVERAGES

*If you're a* New Hampshire native, a frequent visitor, or a fan of snappy, unusual carbonated beverages, then you may have heard of Squamscot Old-Fashioned Beverages. And if not, there's time to remedy that oversight . . .

The Conner family, of Newfields, has been producing and bottling Squamscot Old-Fashioned Beverages for a century and a half, in the same white barn behind the farmhouse on the Conner family farm. The fifth generation of Conners continues the family trade established in 1863 by William H. Conner, whose first tonic was his special "Connermade" spruce beer. In 1911 his son, Alfred, took over, and in 1948, *his* son, Alfred Jr., did the same, returning from the navy in World War II to run the business until 1979. He still lends a hand to the fourth and fifth generations: his son, Tom, and grandson, Dan, as well as longtime employee, Tom Howcroft, all of whom help to keep store shelves filled with batches of award-winning, handcrafted tonic.

*Yankee ingenuity, with a touch of yesteryear: Conner Bottling Works, 120 Exeter Road (Route 85), Newfields; (877) 4NH-SODA; info@nhsoda.com; www.nhsoda.com*

By 1930, the Conners were selling 26,000 cases a year in fourteen flavors, the same year they changed their brand name to Squamscot Beverages. It wasn't until 1938 that Alfred Sr. bought a modern bottling machine. Known as Dixie, she's still doing the job, standing in the same spot in the barn she took all those years ago. Also in the barn, an artesian well pipes in pristine water—one of the reasons the soda tastes so dandy.

Another is the fact that the Conners use only the finest-quality ingredients, including top-shelf syrups, Jamaican ginger, and more. Bottling occurs each afternoon, one flavor at a time, sixty cases an hour—speed aplenty for New Hampshire's last independent bottler, whose products are hands-down some of the tastiest homemade soda pop available today.

Who else makes a soda named "Yup"? How about "Fruit Bowl," "Maple Cream," or "Half and Half"? Or nearly two dozen other tempting flavors, including their energy drink, "Dime Store Pony"? Do they taste as intriguing as they sound? Yup.

# CHUTTERS

*Up in northwest* New Hampshire, close by the Vermont border, Littleton's tony, historic main street is filled with all manner of interesting shops, among them local landmark, Chutters candy store. Famous for one thing—world-famous for it, in fact—Chutters is home to the world's longest candy counter. At 112 feet, you might imagine that it's in the *Guinness Book of World Records* . . . and you'd be correct.

Walking in the front door, you'll be greeted by sweet scents that hang heavy in the air: gumdrops, peppermint swirls, gooey caramels, nutty fudges, and minty, gummy, and cottony confections all mingling to stun the sniffer, muddle the mind, and water the mouth. And most visitors wouldn't trade the sensational assault for anything.

The candy counter is lined with three tiers of big glass jars—more than 800 of them—brimming with colorful, inviting goodies just waiting for visitors to dip in and fill their bags. A number of those jars are packed with nothing but penny candy.

What to choose, what to choose . . . Chutters, 43 Main Street, Littleton; (603)444-5787; www.chutters .com

Chutters has been on Littleton's main street since the late 1800s, when its original owner, Congregational minister Frederick George Chutter, came to town to tend a flock of wayward souls. Instead, he turned his hand to the dry goods business, opening Chutter's General Store. Today, Chutters's sweet offerings literally number in the thousands, and include gummy creatures, jawbreakers, lollipops, licorice, gumballs, and goodies from yesteryear, including Squirrel Nut Zippers, Mint Juleps, Bit-O-Honey, and root-beer barrels. Chutters fudge is only surpassed in flavor by the variety offered (sixteen flavors), and the chocolates include filled truffles, turtles and clusters, dipped pretzels, barks and crunches, even sugar-free chocolates(!).

The only drawback to visiting Chutters is in deciding which glass jar to dive into first. Chutters' customers pay twice by the pound—first with money, then later on, by adding pounds when they indulge in all that gooey goodness, pound after sweet, tasty pound . . . But then again, that's the point of candy, isn't it?

# MOOSE

*Moose* (Algonquin for "eater of twigs"), *Alces alces*, the big bullwinkle, the largest member of the deer family—call them what you will, moose demand to be taken seriously, especially in New Hampshire, where bulls can exceed 1,500 pounds and stand 7 feet tall at the shoulder. They are the largest wild land mammal in the state, and live in all ten New Hampshire counties, though little more than a century ago they were nearly extinct in the Granite State. In fact, by the mid-1800s, fewer than fifteen moose could be found in the state, though at one time they were more common in New Hampshire than white-tailed deer. They didn't really show signs of a comeback until the 1970s, but since then, they have rebounded in surprising numbers statewide—between 5,000 and 6,000—with their biggest population in the Great North Woods.

At a full trot, moose can move up to 35 miles per hour, and are also tremendous swimmers. Only bulls grow antlers, beginning in March or April, shedding them by November, following the "rut,"

Up close and personal: www.mwvmoosetours.com

www.dansscenictours.com

www.outdoorescapesnewhampshire.com

North Country Moose Festival: www.moosefestival.com

or mating season. A full-grown moose can eat forty to sixty pounds of twigs, buds, shrubs, and aquatic plants in a single day. Though they are a hardy breed with a potential life span of twenty years, most moose live little more than a dozen years, due to the debilitating effects of ticks, brainworm, collisions with automobiles (250 each year on New Hampshire's roads), and the October hunting season, which, in the Granite State, reduces the herd by a fraction: In 2011, 395 permits were issued (out of 14,000 applicants).

Moose-watching in New Hampshire is big fun, and one of the best places to spot a bullwinkle is on Moose Alley, a stretch of Route 3 in Pittsburg. Moose should never be approached, however, as they are wild animals and can be deadly dangerous. Despite this, the ungainly ungulates are revered in New Hampshire. Several towns—Colebrook, Canaan, and Pittsburg—collectively hold the annual North Country Moose Festival, featuring moose-spotting, a moose parade, tasty moose burgers, and a moose-calling contest.

# ACKNOWLEDGMENTS

*We wish to thank* the following for their kind assistance during the compilation of this book: our moms, Rose Mary Smith and Gayla Mayo (for enduring our high jinks and shenanigans!); the Smith and the Mayo families; Charity Smith (our Sistah!); Jen and Jeff (and your cool digs!); Guy; Nessie; Erin Turner; Northeast Kingdom Outfitters; Hans Lolkema; NH Highland Games; Kevin Swenson and the staff at Swenson Granite Works; The Robert Frost Farm staff and volunteers; Gary Hildreth/Portsmouth Naval Shipyard and United States Navy; Peta Fifield and her Ayrshire, Pippin; The Deerfield Fair; The Crooked Chimney; Steven Zoldak, Ron Raiselis, and the staff at Strawbery Banke Museum; Mary Ellen and David Dutton, Kim Nedeau, and Leia Fabian at Kellerhaus; Mack's Apples/Moose Hill Orchards; Zhana Morris and The Music Hall; Paula and the staff at the Mill Museum; New Hampshire State House; Everett Bailey, Maisie Daly, and Canterbury Shaker Village; the Brady Family and Six Gun City; President Calvin Coolidge State Historic Site; The MacDowell Colony; the staff at Mt. Monadnock State Park; Kristina Drociak and Stonyfield Farm; Yankee Publishing; Nichole Lederer/NH Motor Speedway; the Hart Family and the staff at Hart's Turkey Farm Restaurant; staff and volunteers at Castle in the Clouds; Dartmouth College; Library of Congress; United States Mint; rock climbers Bruce Althouse Jr. and Tim; Scott Alemany/North Conway Grand Hotel; The League of NH Craftsmen; Nola Grant and the staff at Clark's Trading Post; Laura and the staff at Mount Washington Cog Railway; Gene Ehlert/Mountain View Grand Hotel; Golfers Doug Ferguson and Bill Purdie; Wentworth by the Sea; Tom Howcroft and the Conner Family at Squamscot Beverages/Conner Bottling Works; Tammy and Cat at Chutters; Town of Gorham; and the good folks at The Port Inn.

# PHOTO CREDITS

*All photos* © Jennifer Smith-Mayo except: p. xi, © United States Navy (Portsmouth Naval Shipyard); p. 4, © David and Francis Smith/Northeast Kingdom Outfitters (Francis Smith); p. 17, © United States Navy (top right, USS *Albacore,* bottom right, USS *Greenville,* and bottom left, USS *Dallas*); p. 36, © Library of Congress (Daniel Webster); p. 51, © MacDowell Colony (Alice Walker); © MacDowell Colony/Victoria Sambunaris (picnic hampers); © MacDowell Colony/Bernice Perry (Leonard Bernstein); p. 59, © NHMS/HHP Images (Speedway racing track, Speedway fans); p. 64, © Library of Congress (Robert Frost); p. 74, © United States Mint (Old Man of the Mountain New Hampshire State Quarter); p. 75, © Library of Congress (Old Man of the Mountain).